NATIVE WOMEN AND LAND

Native Women and Land

NARRATIVES OF DISPOSSESSION AND RESURGENCE

STEPHANIE J. FITZGERALD

UNIVERSITY OF NEW MEXICO PRESS • ALBUQUERQUE

© 2015 BY THE UNIVERSITY OF NEW MEXICO PRESS
All rights reserved. Published 2015
Printed in the United States of America
20 19 18 17 16 15   1 2 3 4 5 6

LIBRARY OF CONGRESS CATALOGING-IN-PUBLICATION DATA

Fitzgerald, Stephanie J.
Native women and land : narratives of dispossession and resurgence /
Stephanie J. Fitzgerald.
pages cm
Includes bibliographical references and index.
ISBN 978-0-8263-5557-7 (cloth : alkaline paper) — ISBN 978-0-8263-5558-4
(electronic)
1. Indians of North America—Land tenure. 2. Indian women—North America—
Social conditions. 3. Indian women—Political activity—North America.
4. Environmentalism—North America. 5. Land use—Political aspects—North
America. 6. Land use—Environmental aspects—North America. 7. North
America—Environmental conditions. 8. North America—Ethnic relations.
I. Title.
E98.L3F58 2015
973.04'97—dc23
2014019824

COVER IMAGE © Ryan Young/RM Young Photography (Lac du Flambeau Ojibwe)
COVER MODEL: Myla Garcia (Ohkay Owingeh Pueblo)
BOOK DESIGN: Lila Sanchez

Composed in ScalaOT 10.5/15
Display type is ScalaOT

Timothy P. Fitzgerald

(1939–2012)

CONTENTS

ACKNOWLEDGMENTS

The research and writing of this book were generously supported by the University of Kansas through a New Faculty General Research Fund grant, a General Research Fund grant, and a Haines Faculty Research Fellowship. The American Association of University Women provided welcome support in the form of an American Postdoctoral Fellowship. The Newberry Library granted much-needed research support through a Susan Kelly Power and Helen Hornbeck Tanner Fellowship.

This book would not have come to fruition without the support of family and multiple networks of community. They have sustained me and provided vital support in all sorts of ways during this long journey. There are so many people to thank, and so few pages within which to thank them.

My largest debt is to the late Paula Gunn Allen, mentor, teacher, dear friend, and "auntie," whose teachings and questions continue to influence me today. Michelle Raheja has been a source of inspiration and support from the beginning. Thank you to Hilary Wyss, Kristina Bross, Zabelle Stodolla, Dennis Moore, and the Early American Studies community for your mentorship and friendship. Thank you to my study partners Grace Lee and Michelle Black Wester, who have become lifelong friends. A huge thank-you to Rich Furman for his help with the manuscript. To the Brooks-Kamper family for your unwavering support. Thank you to Betty Donohue for the hospitality and all the good times and to Sally (Miller) Cuaresma and family for their friendship and never-ending hospitality, both in Los Angeles and in Moodys.

At the University of Kansas, Laura L. Mielke has been both a friend and an astute reader of manuscripts. Susan and Billy Joe Harris offered friendship, community, and mentoring. Giselle Anatol has been both sounding board and supporter. Special thanks go to John Edgar Tidwell for the laughs, conversations, and sound advice. Thank you to Byron

Caminero-Santangelo and Doreen Fowler for inspiration and encouragement. Department chairs Dorice Elliot, Marta Caminero-Santangelo, and Anna Neill supported this project in a variety of ways, for which I am profoundly grateful. Thanks also go to the Ad Hoc African/Americanist group for their support and for welcoming me into their community.

In the field of Native American and Indigenous Studies, the critical work of Nehiyaw scholars Janice Acoose, Shawn Wilson, and Margaret Kovach proved to be vital and sustaining. Thank you to Devon Mihesuah for listening. Channette Romero kept me on track and provided needed encouragement. Thank you to Nancy Peterson for your feedback, input, and friendship. To my colleagues in the field of Native and Indigenous Studies Penelope Myrtle Kelsey, Beth H. Piatote, Dory Nason, Laura Furlan, Meg Noodin, and Mike Zimmerman, you are amazing.

A special bosho and shout-out go to the language folks in Mayetta—Billy, Cindy, Pom, Colton, Rencie, Mary and Eddie Joe, Olivia and Robert, Marie, Terri Jo, Joy, Emily, Jessie, Jaden, and Ashley. Igwien.

Elise McHugh, my editor at the University of New Mexico Press, as well as the staff there, has made the editorial and publishing process as smooth as it could possibly be. A special thank-you also goes to Grace B. Labatt for her meticulous copyediting. To the anonymous readers of the manuscript, my most heartfelt thanks.

My family has always been my rock. My parents, Barbara Fitzgerald and Tim and Vicki Fitzgerald, never gave up on me. I only wish my father had lived to see this book in print. My brothers and sisters kept me on my toes by asking if I was still working on the same book. Thank you to Grandma Mary and Aunt Pat for the stories and histories. The Bayhylle and Leading Fox families kept me grounded and laughing. Aunt Gwen Shunatona asked hard questions. Ruth, Alex, and Michael, you three are everything to me; this is for you.

Toward a Land Narrative

ON AN OVERCAST MARCH DAY in Lawrence, Kansas, a group of people gathered on a busy stretch of Thirty-First Street, carrying signs and shouting slogans to passing motorists. They were protesting a proposed bypass extension of the South Lawrence Trafficway through a 573-acre plot of land known as the Wakarusa Wetlands. A few vehicles honked in solidarity, but most rushed by on one of the main arteries that connect the college town of Lawrence with the greater Kansas City area. Despite the collaborative and diverse nature of the group—made up of Indians, whites, and Latinos, students and retirees, families and environmentalists, all mobilized by word of mouth and social media outlets—on this day the group garnered no media attention. As the afternoon grew colder and the skies grayer, the participants packed up their handmade signs and went home.

Most of the forty-odd years during which the proposed bypass extension has been on the table have been marked by environmental impact studies; legal and administrative hearings; and a lawsuit to block construction, filed by six different environmental groups and the Prairie Band Potawatomi Nation, whose reservation lies forty miles northwest of the wetlands. The cause has been taken up over the years by those on both sides of the dispute, including local farmers, landowners, developers, and environmentalists. It has been framed by contentious debates played out in public spaces and in the online readers' forum of the *Lawrence Journal-World*, the local newspaper.

Female protester at the Wakarusa Wetlands near Lawrence, Kansas, March 2011.
Photo by author.

In July 2012, the U.S. Court of Appeals for the Tenth Circuit ruled in favor of the Federal Highway Administration and the Kansas Department of Transportation, giving the green light to build the bypass extension through the Wakarusa Wetlands and seemingly putting an end to the controversy. Public interest in the wetlands issue has now seemed to wane, despite efforts by student environmental groups at Haskell Indian Nations University and the University of Kansas to reframe the narrative of the struggle for the wetlands, shifting it from an environmental issue to a cultural and historical issue. Their efforts have been covered in the Native and alternative media, but not in the local paper. The cause of this apparent disinterest on the part of the general public and local media is unclear. Possibly locals are suffering from "eco-fatigue," exhaustion in the face of one more green spot to worry about and preserve, or it may be that the particular narrative of the plot of land itself is to blame. For as the sign carried by a female protester stated, "This place is soaked in Indian history."[1]

"The history of wetlands," remarks historical geographer Hugh Prince, "is steeped in ideology and rhetoric," and as the brief history related above demonstrates, the Wakarusa Wetlands are no exception.[2] A remnant of the vast network of marsh, wet prairie, and wetland ecosystems that covered the Central Plains for thousands of years, the Wakarusa Wetlands served as a natural stopping place for humans, animals, and bird species on the tallgrass prairies. It remains "one of the most diverse habitats" in the area.[3] In the eighteenth century, the area was the territory of the Kaw, Osage, and Pawnee tribes. In the years prior to the Civil War, the Shawnee, Lenape, Ottawa, Potawatomi, and other tribes forcibly removed from the Old Northwest Territory settled near the waterways and wetlands of eastern Kansas. Today, the 573-acre plot in question abuts the grounds of Haskell Indian Nations University, a former federal Indian boarding school founded in 1884 as the United States Indian Industrial Training Institute. The wetlands formed a part of the Haskell campus until their sale by the federal government in the 1960s to nearby Baker University, as government-owned surplus land.[4] Haskell alumni tell of students using the wetlands as a secret gathering place where they could speak their languages freely, practice ceremonies, and, in the case of runaways, throw government agents off their tracks.[5]

In many ways, and for a very long time, these wetlands have been inscribed as Indian land; they are remembered and recognized as such by Indian people. Their palimpsestic landscape is imprinted with physical, cultural, and spiritual narratives that have retained their resonance throughout the centuries. This is key, for as Keith Basso comments in *Wisdom Sits in Places: Landscape and Language Among the Western Apache*, place-making, or marking land as "Indian," is as much a way of constructing history as it is "a form of *cultural* activity" (emphasis in the original).[6] The cultural activity involved in marking and recognizing the wetlands as Indian land has remained constant since Stephen H. Long's expedition of 1819–1820, which included the first notations of the "Warreruza" River and the Kaw Indian villages in the wetlands' vicinity.[7]

I begin with this specifically local example because as a physical, cultural, and spiritual landscape, the Wakarusa Wetlands function metonymically for other Native American and First Nations landscapes and their attendant narratives and histories of removal and displacement. For the students, alumni, and employees of Haskell Indian Nations University, the wetlands make up part of the cultural and spiritual landscape not only of the campus, but also of the city of Lawrence itself, where I live now.[8] This particular place, this "narrated place-world," is layered with histories of Native and non-Native peoples, of everyday life and ceremonial activity, of joy and tragedy, of Native dispossession and Native resurgence.[9] It is also circumscribed by Anglo-American processes of law and policy that, as of this writing, foretell a bypass that paves over these layered histories and destroys ecosystems.

My personal interest in the Wakarusa Wetlands is connected to another marshland, the Ballona Wetlands of Los Angeles's Westside, where I lived for many years. Driving west at night on Jefferson Boulevard toward the Pacific Ocean, you could hear a choir of bullfrogs and an orchestra of crickets chirping, and you could see fireflies blinking—all courtesy of the wetlands. The Ballona Wetlands are also a stop on the migratory bird Pacific Flyway, and it was not unusual to see egrets or herons rise from the wetlands and head for the estuary to the west. For me personally, as a nehiyaw iskwew, or Cree woman, whose family hails from the waterways of northern Manitoba, the Ballona Wetlands were an Indian space within the city of Los Angeles. They evoked my original landscape, albeit with a different cast of species. This place was imbued with resonance for me, and it was made even more precious when set beside the disruptions in my family's migration story from Cree territory in Manitoba to Southern California: residential school, tuberculosis sanitariums, orphanages, and the eking out of a living through menial labor. Our collective lives were lived near water in its many forms, in different landscapes.

On the bluffs above the Ballona Wetlands is the site of Sa'angna, a Tongva Indian village of the original inhabitants of Los Angeles, occupied by Loyola Marymount University since 1929. There, in the center of campus, the City of Angels Kateri Circle once held its annual intertribal contest powwow in July, in honor of St. Kateri's feast day. The powwow—or dance, as Southern Plains people would call it—drew dancers from all over Los Angeles and Orange Counties, representing tribes from across the country. My children and I participated in these powwows or dances in Southern California, having been introduced to the dance arena through our kinship ties with a Southern Plains family. We still retain our own northern Cree practices and traditions, but when invited to participate in these different cultural practices in a new landscape, we are grateful to our new relations.

Early in the morning, before the activities began, a local Tongva man blessed the ground comprising the dance arena. This is not a Tongva practice; nor are the dances part of Tongva tradition. The man was asked to bless the dance arena as a matter of Native diplomacy and protocol, out of respect for Tongva land. This respect takes the form of honoring the land where we are all visitors, as we have seen by its blessing. We come together in this space that has been transformed by our very presence, out of respect for all of our traditions and for this Indian land. Without active land stewardship, as Native people we will begin to lose our language, our ceremonial and cultural practices, and our land.

Many of the participants in intertribal events such as the powwow I have described arrived in Southern California as a result of the federal government's Indian relocation program, adapting their traditions to a new, urban landscape. These social dances are one way of maintaining cultural and linguistic traditions away from tribal homelands. They are becoming increasingly important as Native people leave reservations for urban areas.[10]

In contrast to the tribes represented within the urban Indian community in Los Angeles, the Tongva are not a federally or state recognized tribe.[11] They have no "official" land base. Their traditional lands encompass both the city and county of Los Angeles, including pricey real estate in Downtown L.A. and Beverly Hills, which has now become private property in the hands of corporations and individuals. The Ballona Wetlands were the last bit of coastal open space on Los Angeles's Westside, making them prime real estate worth a small fortune. Like the Wakarusa Wetlands, the Ballona Wetlands were the subject of a lawsuit that went on for years, before they were finally drained and filled. A luxury subdivision was built on land with a rich narrative of Southern California Indian history.

Some 1,300 miles apart, both the Ballona and Wakarusa wetlands are soaked in Indian history. They provide a layered narrative of Native survivance across the centuries.

Like the wetlands, *Native Women and Land* is mapped onto a landscape that has shifted dramatically over the past fifteen years. Native American and Indigenous Studies as an interdisciplinary field of study has emerged and cohered around a diverse, international group of scholars and the founding of an international academic association.[12] While Native literary studies have taken a dominant tribal nationalist stance since the publication of Robert Warrior's *Tribal Secrets: Recovering American Indian Intellectual Traditions* (1995) and subsequent works by Jace Weaver, Craig Womack, and Daniel Heath Justice, other scholars are looking to forge new links between Native studies and gender studies, postcolonialism, legal studies, and ecocriticism and environmentalism.[13] Of these fields, gender and eco- and environmental criticism have been historically undertheorized in relation to Native studies. As Shari M. Huhndorf points out, "Literary nationalism itself has been a predominantly male endeavor. Nationalist critics have devoted little attention to writing by Native women, especially those works that attend to issues of gender."[14] And as Sue-Ellen Jacobs, Wesley Thomas, and Sabine Lang make clear, "In Native North America, there were and still are cultures in which more than two gender categories are marked."[15] Even less attention has been paid to ecocritical and environmental approaches to Native literary and cultural productions, though we are at a point in time when Native communities are facing environmental crises that threaten their lives and livelihoods, and are being ignored by mainstream media outlets.

Whereas Keith Basso's *Wisdom Sits in Places* is the seminal work on place in the Native American Southwest, full-length studies treating Native literature, ecocriticism, and the environment are few: Joni Adamson's *American Indian Literature, Environmental Justice, and Ecocriticism: The Middle Place* (2001); Donelle N. Dreese's *Ecocriticism: Creating Self and Place in Environmental and American Indian Literatures* (2002); Adamson, Mei Mei Evans, and Rachel Stein's edited volume *The Environmental Justice Reader: Politics, Poetics, and Pedagogy* (2002); and Lee Schweninger's *Listening to the Land: Native American Literary Responses to the Landscape* (2008). In his essay "Toward an Environmental Justice Ecocriticism," included in *The Environmental Justice Reader*, T. V. Reed calls out the field for its lack of attention to questions of race and class, offering suggestions for an environmental justice ecocriticism. And in a 2009 special issue of the journal *MELUS* devoted to "Ethnicity and Ecocriticism," Adamson and Scott Slovic announce a "third wave" ecocriticism that "recognizes ethnic and national particularities and yet transcends ethnic and national boundaries."[16] Ironically, this global turn in the environmental humanities has given scholars further cause to ignore Native American literatures and lands by shifting the focus outside the United States. This is problematic, as many of the multinational corporations involved in environmentally devastating resource extraction around the globe are also operating on U.S. Indian reservations. They rarely make news in the United States.

This book builds upon the work done by the pioneering scholars mentioned above, yet moves beyond it, approaching its subject from a Native-centered and necessarily interdisciplinary perspective and focusing exclusively on Native-authored primary texts for a fuller picture of contemporary Native North America. It extends Basso's work by focusing on tribal nations and communities who either have been removed from their ancestral lands or have experienced substantial land dispossession. In doing so, it addresses a gap in our understanding of the vital role contemporary Native narratives of land and place-making play in the regeneration and resurgence of tribal nations and communities, particularly in the face of ongoing attempts to alienate tribal land bases by means of federal Indian law and policy.

This book is intended to be a step toward defining an American Indian ecocritical and environmental literary practice that is attuned to the complex and ever-shifting relationships Native people have with land tenure and the federal government. As Maureen Konkle explains, "Native peoples' connection to land is not just cultural, as it is usually, and often sentimentally, understood; it is also political—about governments, boundaries, authority over people and territory."[17] Governmental authority refers not just to the federal level; it encompasses tribal laws and regulations as well. To establish an American Indian ecocritical and environmental literary practice is to recognize the inextricability of land tenure, federal Indian law, and environmental issues from the seventeenth century to the present. Twenty-first-century Navajo (Diné) Nation law demonstrates just this:

DINÉ NATURAL LAW DECLARES AND TEACHES THAT:

A. The four sacred elements of life, air, light/fire, water and earth/pollen in all their forms must be respected, honored and protected for they sustain life; and

B. The six sacred mountains, Sisnajini, Tsoodził, Dook'o'oslííd, Dibé Nitsaa, Dził Na'ooditii, Dził Ch'ool'í'í, and all the attendant mountains must be respected, honored and protected for they, as leaders, are the foundation of the Navajo Nation; and

C. All creation, from Mother Earth and Father Sky to the animals, those who live in water, those who fly and plant life have their own laws, and have rights and freedom to exist; and

D. The Diné have a sacred obligation and duty to respect, preserve and protect all that was provided for we were designated as the steward of these relatives through our use of the sacred gifts of language and thinking; and

E. Mother Earth and Father Sky is part of us as the Diné and the Diné is part of Mother Earth and Father Sky; the Diné must treat this sacred bond with love and respect without exerting dominance for we do not own our mother or father.

F. The rights and freedoms of the people to the use of the sacred elements of life as mentioned above and to the use of the land, natural resources, sacred sites and other living beings must be accomplished through the proper protocol of respect and offering and these practices must be protected and preserved for they are the foundation of our spiritual ceremonies and the Diné life way; and

G. It is the duty and responsibility of the Diné to protect and preserve the beauty of the natural world for future generations.[18]

Diné Natural Law is one of four branches of law under the Diné Original Law Structure, along with Traditional Law, Customary Law, and Common Law. These four branches of law were codified in 2002 by a resolution of the Navajo Nation Council amid a "concern that knowledge of these fundamental laws may be fading, especially among young people."[19] The resolution also expresses concern that "this may be a primary reason why the Diné are experiencing many negative forms of behavior and natural events," which would not have occurred if these laws had been observed.[20] To codify Diné Natural Law, rather than import environmental legal language from state or county governments, is to

suggest that tribal codes "must also account for the spiritual and psychological well-being of the collective community as well as individuals."[21] This collective community contains other-than-human entities as
well as humans, who are the stewards of the natural world.

To undertake an attempt to illuminate the complex interplay of
Native land tenure, federal Indian law, and environmental devastation
requires an ethical engagement with Native literary and community
texts, as well as with the Native communities from which they spring.
Such an engagement insists on an interrogation of the stereotypes that
play out in the dominant society and in academic settings—especially
the notion of the ecological Indian. This notion breaks down into other
stereotypes, including those surrounding the ever-popular "Indians are
close to nature" and "close to the land." Such ecological tropes have their
contemporary genesis in an anti-littering "Keep America Beautiful"
campaign public service announcement, shown on television for the
first time on Earth Day, April 22, 1971. The PSA featured character actor
Iron Eyes Cody in nineteenth-century "Indian" attire, paddling a birch
bark canoe past the belching smokestacks of an industrial complex,
then beaching his canoe just feet away from a heavily trafficked highway, only to have a passing motorist throw a bag of trash at his feet. As
Cody surveys the littered and polluted landscape, a single tear runs
down his face. A voice-over intones, "Some people have a deep abiding
respect for the beauty that was once this country. Some people don't."[22]
The PSA immediately set up an oppositional binary between Indian and
non-Indian people, while simultaneously positioning the Indian firmly
in the past as a romanticized "first ecologist." MTV reran the commercial in the 1990s, and it was spoofed on an episode of the animated
series *The Simpsons*, thus cementing the image of the featured actor in
the popular-culture imagination of a new generation. It mattered little
that Cody was not Indian, but an Italian-American born in Louisiana.
For many Americans, he was the only "Indian" they ever saw.[23]

The stereotype of the ecological Indian shows up not only in my university classrooms, but also in articles and books by anthropologists, eco-
critics, and environmentalist scholars. Countering and reversing these

tropes in the classroom and beyond requires tremendous effort and exposure to tribally specific world views, of which the Diné Natural Law is one. Another example comes from Ojibwe scholar Margaret Noori, who explains, "In the notably verb-based language of Anishinaabemowin, no single noun equates with the concept of nature."[24] In an Anishinaabe/Ojibwe context, nature cannot be captured by a single word, but must be represented by a series of morphemes that are linked together relationally, as in the way that human and other-than-human worlds are linked. Noori further notes, "Readers find in older [Anishinaabemowin] texts a concept of nature that encompasses the people's relationship with the land, the trees, the water, and the weather."[25] In short, nature is linked to everything else. The Anishinaabe concept of nature, then, undermines the stereotype of the ecological Indian who is "close to nature" and "close to the land" by expanding what "nature" means. The focus is on relationships, not on sentimental feelings or affinities for what, in American English, can be amorphous concepts. Like the Diné Natural Law, the Anishinaabe/Ojibwe concept of nature rests on relationships and stewardship.

Chickasaw scholar Jodi A. Byrd notes, "For indigenous people, place, land, sovereignty, and memory matter."[26] The words "place," "land," and "memory" evoke strong associations for Native people in North America—as Byrd writes, they *matter*. For those both on and away from their tribal homelands, those words conjure up memories of particular landscapes, of what *happened* there. Both the Ballona and Wakarusa wetlands examples evoke what *happened* on those sites, and *how* such occurrences *matter* to indigenous people. As Basso explains, such memories are "pointedly local and unfailingly episodic."[27] Memory is evoked in similar ways in Diné poet Esther G. Belin's poem "Directional Memory," in which the speaker recalls, "Indian land was far away in another world, across state lines . . . / . . . I always forget LA has sacred mountains."[28] Belin grew up in Los Angeles County, but she has written about making frequent car trips back to the Navajo reservation during her childhood. These lines from "Directional Memory" are particularly interesting as they bring into play both the six sacred mountains of

Dinetah, the Navajo homeland, and the mountains surrounding Los Angeles. The latter are sacred to local tribes, who are not mentioned by name in the poem. The lines reinforce the particularity of memory of Diné space, while simultaneously unsettling the Native space of the speaker's new place/land, although the speaker's new place is ultimately acknowledged as "sacred" space as well.

While "place" is more easily and more frequently invoked, as in an "Indian place," the term "Indian land" carries with it a plethora of meanings: home, return, removal, displacement, dispossession, and trust land. As a legal term enshrined in the U.S. Code, it can mean individually or tribally owned land, trust land, or restricted fee land. The term quickly spirals into a confusing subset of different definitions for the different branches of the U.S. Department of the Interior, of which the Bureau of Indian Affairs is a part. "Indian land" has its own set of initials and descriptors: BLM (Bureau of Land Management) land, lease land, graze land. Then there is the "income" it generates in the form of Individual Indian Money (IIM) accounts, the gross mismanagement of which was the subject of the 1996 landmark class action lawsuit *Cobell v. Salazar, et al.*[29] Given all of this, it is not surprising that Cherokee scholar Jace Weaver has noted, "Aside from his or her relation to family, clan, or tribal nation, an Indian's most significant relationship is with the federal government."[30] This relationship governs not only where we live, but it also determines the actual houses we live in (the infamous HUD houses), the food we eat (commodities, anyone?), and the health care and education we receive. In short, the federal government has its hands in every aspect of Indian life, and that intrusion stems from a long history of defining, codifying, and subsuming "Indian land."

The flip side of "Indian land" is "Indian Country," a charged term with multiple connotations. When used to denote an "Indian place," the term is expressed with affection by Native people, as in, "It's good to be back in Indian Country." It also figures in the title of a major Indian newspaper, *Indian Country Today*. Yet the term also resonates with imperialist and colonialist discourse. It was first used by England in the Royal Proclamation of 1763, which prohibited the settlement of colonists west of the Appalachian Mountains—an area that remained "Indian Country." The U.S. Congress defines "Indian Country" in the U.S. Code (18 U.S.C. 1151) as reservation land, dependent Indian communities, and all Indian allotments, assuming Indian title has not been extinguished.[31] For most Americans, however, the meaning of "Indian Country" continues to be the military definition of "enemy territory." First used by U.S. Cavalry troops in the nineteenth century to designate Indian-occupied lands, "Indian Country" was resurrected during the Vietnam War to denote Viet Cong territory, and again during the Iraq War, coloring the shades of meaning given to a place Indian people designate as home. These disruptions to the meaning and relationships that entwine Indian land have a long history in the United States. They must be examined alongside any discussion of Native people and their relationship to their environment.

Native Women and Land examines representations, primarily by Native women, of land loss, dispossession, and environmental devastation in contemporary literature, community texts such as newsletters and informational brochures, and social media. These forms of loss, dispossession, and devastation have been brought about in part by federal Indian law and policy. Native land dispossession enacted through government legislation—including presidential order, forced removal, allotment, and eminent domain—and climate change have impacted tribal nations and communities since the early nineteenth century, and they continue to do so into the twenty-first century. Thus dispossession is not just a legal or land tenure issue; it becomes an environmental issue as well.

I choose to focus on Native women's representations, narratives, and experiences of land dispossession and environmental devastation in part because of the paucity of scholarship on the subject. Joni Seager points out that "[d]isaster is seldom gender neutral," and as I argue, the same goes for dispossession.[32] Women and children suffered disproportionately during Hurricane Katrina in 2005. Even as I write, the nightly news shows refugee camps in the Middle East and Africa full of women and children who are dependent on food rations from the Western world. (These rations come from the United States and are often the same "commodities" supplied to American Indians.) In a Native context, most histories of removal and dispossession have tended to focus on men, and especially on male leaders who opposed removal. As Wendy Harcourt and Arturo Escobar note, "Too often the differences between men and women become smoothed away. Knowledge about women continues to become the hardest to come by."[33] Similarly, knowledge about Native people is also difficult to come by. It is the effort *not* to smooth away the differences between male and female experiences, and between Native and non-Native experiences of dispossession, that forms the impetus for this book.

While some instances of Native dispossession and removal, such as the Cherokee Removal of 1838–1839, are familiar to many, accounts of incremental and accretive dispossessions—such as those caused by thawing permafrost or permanently frozen subsoil in the Arctic, or by soil erosion in coastal areas (a result of rising sea levels)—are virtually ignored. This book asks: How are these forms of dispossession, both sudden and incremental, experienced by Native people? How are these experiences shaped by gendered concerns? What roles do literary and community texts and social media play in the memory, politics, and lived experience of those dispossessed? More important, what happens after dispossession?

Native Women and Land offers possible answers to these questions, but it also raises other important questions. What would happen to the study of literature and the environment if we were to move Native American literature from the extreme periphery, where it now resides, to the center? How would readings of Native-focused ecocriticism and environmental literature change if Native people were no longer part of the landscape, but were instead leading the discussions? The first question, of course, has its own genealogy, going back to Mary Helen Washington's presidential address to the American Studies Association in 1997, "Disturbing the Peace: What Happens to American Studies If You Put African American Studies at the Center?"[34] Shari M. Huhndorf has recently reprised this question, asking, "What happens to American studies if you put Native studies at the center?"[35] The question I pose, then, is not a new one, but rather one that belongs to a trajectory of similar questions regarding the place of ethnic studies, especially Native studies in academia. It is a difficult one to answer, as an answer would require shifts in the critical terrain of the field of literature and the environment, which has only recently incorporated multiethnic and world literatures into its canon. Part of the answer lies in the decolonization of this field, which has been raced and gendered white and male and constructed over Indian land and Indian bodies. To include Native American texts in the field of literature and the environment requires a recognition that federal law played a role in creating what some refer to as pristine wilderness areas, by depopulating these places of their original Native American inhabitants. *Everywhere you go in North America is Native land.*

In order to write about this, to enter into the scholarly conversation that has tended to ignore the presence of Native people and Native land, it is necessary to link together fields of study across disciplinary lines: literary studies, Native studies, environmental studies, and federal Indian law and policy. By placing literary texts in proximity with case studies of Native and indigenous dispossession and resurgence across academic disciplines, I align myself with Dakota scholar Elizabeth Cook-Lynn, who forcefully argues, "Literature can and does successfully contribute to the politics of possession and dispossession."[36] In other words, literature *matters* when we talk about Native land tenure and dispossession, and vice versa. It is impossible to talk about land tenure issues without taking into consideration issues of law, policy, and environmental justice. It is narrative that creates the representation of the dispossessed, challenges the hegemonic invisibility of Native land dispossession in all its forms, and disseminates potentially useful and strategic counternarratives.

In my analyses of the texts I consider here, I draw on a framework of what I identify as *land narratives*. Land itself has its own story—one rooted in tribally specific creation stories—which is embedded in and retold in every subsequent Native narrative. These land narratives are made legible through landscapes, waterways, and other geographic features, in addition to plant and animal life; all are imbued with spiritual power and indigenous knowledge. This framework allows me to interrogate not only contemporary literary, social media, and community texts by women, but also the ways in which gender and federal Indian law have shaped how Native communities created—and continue to create—land narratives in response to removal, allotment, and other forms of land dispossession. New land narratives are reflected in their literary and textual responses, which in turn become both part of the land narrative tradition and themselves new land narratives. Although rooted in traditional stories, they encompass new events and new experiences, and they are embedded in the accretive structure of the land narrative. The texts I address in this book also form part of the land narrative tradition.

There is a trajectory, then, of land narratives that are continuously created and re-created, from creation stories to contemporary literature. Taken together, they map out the continuance of Native peoples and nations in the face of continuing land loss and dispossession.

An example is in order. In what follows, I retell and analyze two Ojibwe creation stories as representations of original land narratives.

THE ORIGINAL LAND NARRATIVES, OR, TWO STORIES OF CREATION

Kitchi-Manitou created the world and everything in it. But as this world came to an end, it flooded with water. At the same time, changes were happening in the upper world. Sky Woman was married to a Manitou there, and was filled with new life. The birds and animals in the flooded world below clung to the tops of trees and mountains, watching as Sky Woman's belly grew and she became tired and weary. They invited Sky Woman to come down to their world and rest on Turtle's back.

Once she had settled in, Sky Woman asked for a handful of earth. One by one, the animals volunteered to dive down into the floodwaters, and one by one, they emerged empty-handed. Finally, the muskrat poked his head up through the waters, gasping for breath, and in his tightly clutched paw was a tiny ball of mud. Sky Woman took this ball of mud and rubbed it around the edge of turtle's back, blowing on it all the while, and the mud grew into a huge island. Only then did Sky Woman give birth to twins.

In yet another story, Nanaboozhoo found himself stranded on a mountaintop when the waters suddenly began to rise. He hitched a ride on a drifting log, which he shared with small animals and resting birds. Nanaboozhoo prayed to the Manitous, but the waters continued to rise. Suddenly, he remembered that Sky Woman had saved the earth from flooding once before. He called out to the animals to dive down to the bottom of the floodwaters for a handful of mud. One by one, they dove down into the water, and one by one, they emerged empty-handed. Once again, it was the muskrat that emerged with a tiny ball of mud in his paw. Nanaboozhoo breathed into the ball of mud as Sky Woman once did, and it grew, covering the log where he drifted, creating an island that soon formed a new world with mountains and valleys, rivers and lakes, forests and meadows.[37]

These two Ojibwe stories of creation and regeneration form part of a long indigenous narrative tradition that details the creation of worlds and the emergence of the People. The stories depict worlds in transition, always already in existence, and constantly in motion. Underpinning the narratives are deep pedagogical and epistemological functions; the stories serve as systems of knowledge for their communities. But they resonate on other registers as well. They show us that Turtle Island, or North America, is Indian land, demonstrating a Native presence that predates the waves of fishermen, explorers, and settlers that engulfed the continent. They depict a relationship to land based on kinship structures, collaboration, and stewardship, rather than on Western forms of capitalism and commodification. These narratives are not just "long ago" stories. They are vibrant narratives that continue to be retold, reinvented, and redeployed within tribal communities into the twenty-first century, as the sheer variety of the forms these stories take attests.[38]

The gendered nature of the Sky Woman narrative—in which a woman takes charge of the regeneration of the world and its landscape—is richly textured and multilayered. Sky Woman's roles as wife and expectant mother do not restrict her to the upper world, where her husband resides. She responds quickly to the environmental crises at hand by collaborating with the animals, thereby re-creating the world. Sky Woman is a life-giving force, both as a pregnant woman and then as one who gives birth to twins (also an example of fecundity) immediately after the world is re-created. It is an Indian world she re-creates.

Nanaboozhoo's narrative belongs to a cycle of stories in which he steals fire, tricks other animals, at times disguises himself as a female, and generally disrupts the world's order.[39] He can usually be found in precarious situations, as in the above story of the sudden flood. But he always finds a way out, restoring order and imparting some gift to the People, whether it is the variegated bark of birch trees or the medicinal willow tree. In the flood narrative, he regenerates the world by recalling the prior story of Sky Woman, suggesting that he, too, listens to stories and learns from them.

Both stories are examples of a world in environmental crisis, as exemplified by the flood. In today's context, they can be read as allegories of climate change. As such, they move beyond mere entertainment, offering important lessons about land stewardship and collaboration with others. They suggest that environmental degradation is not inevitable. Through an ethic of reciprocity and collaboration, regeneration of the land is possible. Such an ethic is embedded in Anishinaabe storytelling. Noori explains, "As we explore the way the Anishinaabe speak and write about nature, it is important to keep in mind the way the Anishinaabe traditionally tell stories; it is to ask 'Aanii gaa ezhiwebag? What happened? What did the animals and people do?'"[40] The presence and interaction of the animals in the two stories remind the listener/reader of the relationship he or she has with them. In Anishinaabe or

Ojibwe cosmology, animals serve as clan markers, or dodems, further cementing the bond between human and other-than-human beings. They illustrate the interdependence of human and nonhuman entities, and they depict a relationship to land that is based on kinship, reciprocity, and stewardship. Within these stories, the cosmos is ordered in such a way that humans, animals, plant life, and landscape are entwined in a manner that is at once complex and understandable.

By participating in the storytelling process, as listeners and audience members, the community creates meaning and personal expression from the narratives. These meanings and expressions are then incorporated into local indigenous knowledge forms.

As these two Ojibwe creation stories suggest, for Native and indigenous peoples, everything begins and ends with land. It is the subject of the original narratives that, as Taiaiake Alfred points out, contain the "original instructions" for life.[41] Land functions as a microcosm of the Native world, which is re-created again and again through each retelling of the creation story. Just as the earth on the turtle's back grew into North America, Native communities came into being throughout the continent through their own individual origin stories and their own individual landscapes. Each particular landscape, each geographic formation has its unique attendant stories, whether they be those of the narrated place-worlds of the Cibecue Apache or writer Simon Ortiz's stories of Acoma Pueblo, North America's oldest continuously inhabited community, the setting for his poetry, fiction, and prose writings.

This book is divided into two sections, Askîy/Land and Nîpîy/Water. These mark two different forms of Native dispossession. While Native and indigenous peoples have been dispossessed of both land and waterways, as we move into the twenty-first century, water as a discrete form has become a means of land dispossession on its own. Land and water are also symbols of endurance, of the resurgence and regeneration of Native nations, and they figure prominently in the creation narratives discussed earlier in this introduction. They are also nonrenewable resources, and as such they require care and stewardship, just as the original stories do.

The contemporary novels, poems, and social media and community texts I examine focus on different historical periods, but all revolve around themes of land loss and environmental devastation as shaped by federal Indian law and policy. The first chapter centers on the Cherokee Removal and the Navajo Long Walk of the nineteenth century, perhaps the defining moments in their respective tribal histories. I consider a range of texts, including Diane Glancy's novel *Pushing the Bear: A Novel of the Trail of Tears* (1996), its sequel *Pushing the Bear: After the Trail of Tears* (2009), and Luci Tapahonso's poem "In 1864," placing them in dialogue with extraliterary sites—such as the Cherokee Heritage Center, with its permanent exhibit on the Trail of Tears, and the Bosque Redondo Memorial—in order to answer the question of what happens to a people's land narratives when those people are forcibly and traumatically removed to a new landscape. In chapter 2, the focus shifts to the deforestation of Louise Erdrich's fictional North Dakota reservation as a result of the General Allotment Act of 1887 (also known as the Dawes Act). This is explored through a juxtaposition of Erdrich's novels *Tracks* and *Four Souls*. I argue that Erdrich's fictional characters create new land narratives in response to the encroachment on and erosion of the bounded space of the reservation, caused by allotment and the influence of lumber-industry interests. Originally inscribed on Anglo-American maps intended to delineate where dispossession began and ended, the bounded spaces of the reservations have now become home spaces that must be defended and preserved.

The third chapter takes on Native land dispossession caused by federal policies of eminent domain, as well as the effects on lifeways and the natural landscape of events such as the construction of hydroelectric dams along the Missouri River in the United States and James Bay in Canada, and the subsequent flooding of Native lands. Such phenomena change the narrative between the People and their land. The concluding chapter looks at climate change as the process of indigenous removal for the twenty-first century, exploring case studies of very different Native nations facing similar environmental circumstances: the United Houma Nation of Louisiana and the Alaska Native villages of Kivalina and Shishmaref. All three battle coastal erosion and rising sea levels caused by a complex interplay of circumstances that are literally washing their lands and livelihoods away. In all three cases, members of these nations have turned to social media outlets such as YouTube and Facebook in order to disseminate to a worldwide audience information about their struggles with the effects of climate change and resource extraction. This is a new form of storytelling. Finally, the conclusion examines the impact of the Canadian First Nations movement Idle No More, started by four women and a Twitter hashtag. Ignited by government legislation that in part lifted environmental protection from Canada's numerous lakes, rivers, streams, and other waterways, Idle No More has united First Nations peoples across Canada and has gained allies around the world.

Through its examination of Native American literary, community, and social media texts, *Native Women and Land* intervenes in current environmental and ecocritical approaches to Native American and indigenous literatures, in order to make explicit the ways in which land dispossession, environmental crises, and federal Indian law are deeply entwined. Recognizing these entwined relationships is the first step toward a new Native environment-centered scholarship.

ASKÎY / LAND

CHAPTER ONE

Removals and Long Walks

... and we walked.

—DIANE GLANCY, *Pushing the Bear: A Novel of the Trail of Tears*

LAND NARRATIVES ARE EMBEDDED IN Native languages and world views. Okanagan writer Jeannette Armstrong notes, "Our word for the land is tmxwulaxw. If broken down to determine meaning, the word is made up of two images: tmxw is a shortened version of tmixw (life force of the land) and ulaxw (the physical earth)."[1] The word "tmxwulaxw" describes an animated landscape that is life-giving and -sustaining. She goes on to explain:

> In my Okanagan Nsyilxcen language, the word Kwtlakin? is an Okanagan question phrase that I believe exemplifies the connection between Land/Language-Literature and Identity. . . . The question "Kwtlakin, *What is your place?*" is a vastly different question than . . . *where do you live?* This is a phrase used to "Place" an individual. Instead of asking one "where are you from?" or "who are you?," the question seeks to "Place" you within a context of the land's story.[2]

Knowing one's "place" within "the land's story" is part of being at home in Indian Country or on Indian land, and this knowledge forms the essence of the land narrative framework. Because of the colonial relationship of Native nations with the U.S. and Canadian governments, the "places" within "the land's stories" have become disrupted by a myriad of factors, including forced removals, relocations, and environmental crises. Relationships with these place-worlds are complex, and their histories vary between tribal groups, as Leslie Marmon Silko delineates:

> One of the other advantages that we Pueblos have enjoyed is that we have always been able to stay with the land. Our stories cannot be separated from their geographical locations, from actual physical places on the land. We were not relocated like so many Native American groups who were torn away from their ancestral land. And our stories are so much a part of these places that it is almost impossible for future generations to lose them—there is a story connected with every place, every object in the landscape.[3]

It is precisely because the Pueblo people, like the Cibecue Apache about whom Keith Basso writes, were not removed from their original lands that their stories remain with them. The stories Silko refers to, called into existence by their attachment to place, have been told and retold for generations by the people of the Laguna Pueblo, and in Silko's case, they have also taken the form of the written word in physical books. No matter what form the stories take, they are part of a land narrative.

Native people who are removed to unfamiliar locations must incorporate their original stories into new land narratives, literally re-placing themselves in a new land by creating new stories. This chapter focuses on the literary and cultural productions arising out of the dispossession and forced removal of two very different Native nations, with different landscapes and histories: the Cherokee and the Diné (Navajo). With dispossession and forced removal comes a disruption in each nation's land narratives. Much as the Cherokee and Diné made accommodations to these disruptions, changes and accommodations have been made to their land narratives.

The Cherokee National Holiday is held every year on Labor Day weekend in Tahlequah, the capital of the Cherokee Nation of Oklahoma, to commemorate the September 6, 1839, signing of the Constitution of the Cherokee Nation. The principal chief gives a state of the nation address; there are softball tournaments, a rodeo, and a two-day intertribal pow-wow; and the Cherokee Heritage Center waives its admissions fee. Hotel rooms are booked a year in advance, restaurants are overflowing, and the streets are crowded with cars bearing out-of-state license plates and tribal tags. It is a time to visit family and friends, to be at home in Cherokee Country.

It is also a time for remembering, for this holiday commemorates the end of the "Trail Where We Cried" and the resurgence of the Cherokee Nation in Indian Territory through the signing of the nation's constitution by George Lowrey, president of the National Convention of the Cherokee Nation. The Cherokee National Holiday also marks this place, Tahlequah, as the Cherokee land where the "Eastern and Western Cherokees have again reunited, and become one body politic, under the style and title of the Cherokee Nation."[4] The holiday celebrates the successful placement of the Cherokee people in a new landscape. On a less conspicuous register, it commemorates the journey of the Trail itself, which becomes part of the land narrative.

When visiting friends in the rural Cherokee community of Moodys for the holiday, I drive in to town to visit the Cherokee Heritage Center. The heritage center occupies an interesting space within the Cherokee Nation of Oklahoma. It "functions as a tribal museum," yet it was built on state land in 1963 by the Cherokee National Historical Society.[5] Though the historical society is not part of the Cherokee Nation, it serves as the repository for the Cherokee Nation Archive, and two seats on its executive board are reserved for tribal members, with the principal chief and deputy chief as ex officio members. The Cherokee Heritage Center was built on the space formerly occupied by the Cherokee Female Seminary. The National Park Service has also designated the historical society as an interpretive site for the western end of the Trail of Tears.[6] It lies *within* the nation's boundaries, in Park Hill, yet it is not *of* the nation. It bears the responsibility of representing the history of the Cherokee Nation in Oklahoma.

The center itself is part of a large complex comprising a museum and gift shop, a genealogical center, a 1700s-era ancient village, and a replica of an 1890s settlement. It is the museum's permanent exhibit on the Trail of Tears that captures my attention, as it does that of the many other people making their way through the center on this hot September afternoon. The exhibit occupies six galleries depicting the six stages of Cherokee nationhood: pre-Removal, the court battles leading up to Removal, Removal (the focus of three galleries), and, in the final gallery, the rebuilding of the nation.

The largest of the galleries is the fifth, which has an interactive exhibit with several figures—men, women, and children—cast in white and lit from within. Each tells his or her story of the Trail. Some stories belong to well-known figures in Cherokee history, such as John Ross, principal chief of the Cherokee Nation from 1822 to 1866. Others belong to survivors of the Trail, such as Rebecca Neguin, whose story is given voice by a modern-day tribal member:

> They drove us out of our house to join other prisoners in a stockade. After they took us away, my mother begged them to let her go back and get some bedding. So they let her go back and she brought what bedding and a few cooking utensils she could carry and had to leave behind all of our other household possessions.[7]

Other stories come from the community at large, such as the following, told in the voice of Cherokee tribal member Mary Tidwell in a 2000 recording:

> There was one woman who gave birth to a little baby girl while she was on the Trail. But the difficulties of childbirth and the hardships of the Trail were too much for her, and she died. The baby was cared for and carried the rest of the way by her sister. The baby survived and lived to an old age. She was my great-great-grandmother.[8]

I am particularly drawn to this portion of the interactive exhibit because it tells family stories of nunna dual tsuny, or, literally, the "Trail Where We Cried."[9] The Tidwell story also highlights the perils of dispossession for women and children discussed in the introduction. Dispossession is seldom gender neutral; nor is it age-neutral. In other words, women, the very young, and the elderly are disproportionately impacted by acts of dispossession such as the Cherokee Removal of 1838–1839. The exhibit and the stories it contains are just one facet of Cherokee Removal. There are as many stories as there were people on the forced marches, who came from the Eastern Band of Cherokee in North Carolina and the two Oklahoma tribes, the Cherokee Nation of Oklahoma and the United Keetoowah Band.

The vast majority of the Trail narratives are family stories that, according to Cherokee scholar Betty Booth Donohue, are closely held within the family unit and are not divulged to strangers.[10] This is not surprising, as Carolyn Ross Johnston writes that "[o]ral histories of the Trail of Tears are filled with images of . . . trauma."[11] In contrast, Barbara Duncan explains, "Many families tell stories about how they came to be part of the Eastern Band instead of being taken to Oklahoma in the Removal. Although these events happened in 1838, they are told as though they happened yesterday."[12] For example, Edna Chekelele of the Eastern Band of Cherokee relates:

> There was a basket that was give to me in Oklahoma . . . that's over a hundred and fifty years old, and it's still good and sturdy, and it's a white oak basket that went on the Trail of Tears. No telling how many people have died in front of this basket. If this basket could talk to you, there's no telling what all it would tell you that happened along the Trail of Tears.[13]

Chekelele's basket has its own set of stories, which are hinted at but not revealed in the particular context in which this excerpt was told. They may be family or clan stories—a form of cultural or intellectual property just as the basket is. Chekelele's description of the basket as a storied, animate object is powerful. It takes on new and deeper meanings in the context of the Trail, and as a gift from an Oklahoma Cherokee to an Eastern Band Cherokee.

While material items such as baskets survived the Trail, very few written accounts exist. Though some letters from Cherokees walking the Trail are extant, Vicki Rozema notes that "most surviving accounts of the removal were written by white men."[14] Arnold Krupat points out that despite high literacy rates within the Cherokee Nation in both the Cherokee and English languages, there are no contemporaneous Cherokee-authored accounts of the Trail. He asks, "How to represent such horror?"[15] For those who survived, the answer may have been that one simply doesn't.

The *Trail of Tears Exhibit* at the Cherokee Heritage Center is the largest in the museum. The size of the exhibit and the space devoted to it, according to Hochunk museum scholar Amy Lonetree, demonstrate how it works in "shaping the public perceptions of [Cherokee] past."[16] The Cherokee tribe is possibly the most well-known Native nation in the United States, due in large part to the Trail of Tears and its multivalent representations. Such representations of the Trail are not only to be found in Oklahoma, however. The Cherokee Historical Association in Cherokee, North Carolina, has been running its outdoor drama *Unto These Hills* since 1950. Its website describes the family-friendly drama: "From the first contact with Europeans to the infamous and tragic Trail of Tears, *Unto These Hills* tells the triumphant story of the Cherokee through the eons."[17] In examining these heritage sites, it becomes evident that the Trail of Tears takes precedence over all other Cherokee historical events, making it the defining moment in Cherokee tribal history.

One can also drive (or walk) along the National Park Service's Trail of Tears National Historic Trail, which follows the original route of the Cherokee Removal over land and water, through nine states. The NPS offers a free twenty-two-minute video, made in collaboration with the Cherokee Nation; the video covers the Trail of Tears and the "Cherokee people's determined struggle to maintain their cultural identity."[18] The NPS website mentions the removal of five other tribes during this time, but it does not mention them by name. Nor are they highlighted as prominently as are the Cherokee.

Though many Indian nations were forcibly removed from their homelands during the antebellum period, the Cherokee experience is seared into the public consciousness.[19] It is the only removal the average person remembers. Theda Perdue and Michael D. Green offer an explanation as to why this might be:

> [T]here are reasons why scholars have so frequently told the story of Indian removal in Cherokee terms. One is that the debate over removal policy that occurred in the press, various public settings, and Congress focused on the Cherokees. The laws, treaties, and historical examples cited as the discussions progressed always related to the Cherokees. . . . [T]he Cherokee leaders . . . were uniquely well educated and extraordinarily articulate in both spoken and written English. In countless public speeches and written statements, they produced a trove of documents that dwarfs the records of other Native nations. They were also masters of public relations. Their policy was to make certain that no one could forget them.[20]

As the museum exhibits, living-history displays, and pageantry suggest, the Cherokee Trail of Tears has not been forgotten—not by historians, legal scholars, or popular culture. Scholarly books are still written on the Cherokee Trail of Tears, artists and sculptors still craft imaginative representations, and legal scholars and Indian law practitioners still rely on the Marshall Trilogy—*Johnson v. M'Intosh* (1823), *Cherokee Nation v. Georgia* (1831), and *Worcester v. Georgia* (1832)—which led up to removal and which forms the bedrock of federal Indian law. The Cherokee would seem to be, as Maureen Konkle puts it, "everybody's Indians."[21]

In the latter half of the twentieth century, Cherokee and other novelists have taken up their pens to write fictional accounts of the Trail.[22] Despite the prominence of the Cherokee Trail of Tears in the American public consciousness, fictional accounts are few. Including children's literature—and one romance novel—the total number of published

Trail fictional works is somewhere around twenty. Most are by non-Cherokee authors.[23] This raises questions of intellectual property: To whom do these stories of the Trail belong, and who can tell them or write about them? Do they fall within the purview of individuals, families, clans, or the three Cherokee tribes, individually or collectively?

In this opening chapter, I turn to Diane Glancy's pair of novels *Pushing the Bear: A Novel of the Trail of Tears* (1996) and *Pushing the Bear: After the Trail of Tears* (2009), reading them through a land narrative framework. I ask two main questions: What happens to a people's land narratives when those people are forced to move to a new landscape? Or, to put it another way, what happens to their stories?

There are as many versions of the Cherokee creation story as there are tellers of the tale. It exists in written form in books by James Mooney, Theda Perdue and Michael D. Green, Barbara Duncan, and Christopher Teuton. It survived the Trail and continues to be told by all three bands of the Cherokee Nation. It begins with water and Galunlati, the Sky World, where the animals lived. Galunlati was crowded, and the animals needed more room. They were also curious about what lay below the water. Dayunisi, Beaver's Grandchild, the water beetle, volunteered for the mission. He dove to the bottom and came back with a handful of mud. The mud began to grow and form the earth, Elohi. The earth was soft and wet. It needed to dry before the animals could come down from the Sky World. The Great Buzzard flew down to see if the earth was ready, but he grew tired when he came to Cherokee Country. His wings flapped and dragged on the ground, creating mountains and valleys.[24]

Like the Ojibwe creation story discussed in the introduction, the Cherokee story begins with water, and animals figure prominently in the creation of a specifically Cherokee landscape. This land, with its unique geographic formations of rivers, mountains, and caves, and with its diverse array of plants and animals, is suffused with spiritual power.[25] The creation story is linked to other Cherokee stories that detail the creation of the first humans out of clay, as well as the story of Selu, the Corn Mother. The Cherokee Nation rests on a storied landscape that forms the center of Cherokee cosmology. These stories also inform Glancy's novels.

As Daniel Heath Justice has commented, the subtitle of the first *Pushing the Bear* novel, *A Novel of the Trail of Tears*, suggests that this is neither the only novel on the subject, nor the only account.[26] Moreover, the subtitle reminds us that not all Cherokee walked the Trail. John Ross's contingent traveled by boat from Ross's Landing, now known as Chattanooga, Tennessee. Others stayed behind, hiding in the woods or in caves in North Carolina. Yet others walked the Trail, then turned around and walked right back to North Carolina.[27] There is no single authoritative Trail experience.

Glancy brings together fictional characters and their experiences of the Trail with historical figures and documents. The result is a poly-vocal narrative (with forty-one different voices) informed by both voice and movement. The first *Pushing the Bear* opens with a map of the northern route of the Cherokee Removal, from Cherokee Agency in North Carolina through Tennessee, Kentucky, Illinois, Missouri, and Arkansas, and finally to Fort Gibson, Oklahoma. The book is organized into chapters bearing place-names and sections of the Trail's map. Like the fragments of the pieced-together pottery bowl that Glancy discusses in her author's note, these pieces of map form a coherent whole when read together—just as the disparate voices form a coherent whole of the nunna dual tsuny, or Trail Where We Cried. Glancy recounted in an interview that while writing *Pushing the Bear*, she "realized we are a multiplicity of voices. Each voice has its own words, and you have to listen to the whole group to understand."[28]

Pushing the Bear recounts the Trail experiences of many Cherokee characters, but the principal voice is that of Maritole, a young Cherokee woman, expressed as she interacts with her husband, Knobowtee, and, to a lesser extent, their families and neighbors. The action of the novel is immediate: as Maritole sits on the cabin steps with her baby, her husband walks into the clearing flanked by soldiers with rifles and bayonets.

Removal has begun by the first page. Since Maritole's first few words in the novel are represented in the Cherokee syllabary, only those privileged readers with Cherokee literacy can understand the depth of her anguish. Knobowtee's speech is presented in English, although he speaks "in our language."[29] He tells Maritole, "We'll march . . . Chief John Ross hoped we could keep our land. But Ridge and Boudinot, the leaders in Georgia, signed the treaty that took our land away."[30] This immediate plunge into talk of treaties and land cessions frames Glancy's two novels as "mobilizing" what Chadwick Allen terms "treaty discourse."[31] Treaty discourse continues through both novels, as characters debate the long line of treaties the Cherokee have negotiated, first with the British and then with the U.S. government. Knobowtee's dialogue references the 1835 Treaty of New Echota, which divided the Cherokee into Treaty Party and National Party factions, just as the Trail will divide Maritole and Knobowtee.

Maritole's reaction to the soldiers' orders is directed toward her home landscape: "They couldn't remove us. Didn't the soldiers know we were the land? The cornstalks were our grandmothers. In our story of corn, a woman named Selu had been murdered by her sons. Where her blood fell, corn grew. The cornstalks waved their arms trying to hold us."[32] This initial mention of a significant figure in Cherokee cosmology occurs on the second page of text, beginning the land narrative out of sequence. The story of Selu is oriented toward the beginning of the Cherokee as a people and their world, not the end of their known world. There are numerous references to corn in these first few pages of removal, demonstrating the centrality of corn and its narratives to the Cherokee: "the dried cornstalks in the field by the cabin," "the woods beyond the cornfield whirled," "I walked sideways and fell into the cornstalks at the side of the road."[33] These references foreshadow the journey to come and highlight the role stories can play in the survival and regeneration of a people. Maritole carries stories and memories of landscape with her as she leaves with Knobowtee and the soldiers, still clutching the apple core from her orchard.

In a scene reminiscent of Rebecca Neugin's Trail story from the Cherokee Heritage Center, the soldiers allow a group of women to go back to their cabins for cooking pots and bedding.[34] Knobowtee instructs Maritole to retrieve bags of seed corn, his musket, and some bedding. When she arrives at her cabin, she finds "[w]hite people at [her] table."[35] Maritole returns to the camp with bedding, an iron kettle, and, because of a confrontation with the squatters, burns on both hands. Knobowtee turns away from her as she tries to explain her failure to bring the seed corn and musket, left behind in the cabin when the soldiers hurried her away following the confrontation. Both are devastated by the loss of land, home, and identity. Without a musket and seed corn, Knobowtee can no longer provide for or protect his family. For Maritole, the loss may well run deeper. Cherokee women own the land, the cabins, and the fields. She mourns for both the land and the material things passed down: "bowls and the bone-handled forks. . . . [The] bone-carved hairpin. . . . The feather-edged dishes. . . . My garden beside the cabin bordered with blue columbine. The peach and apple trees. The fields and sky."[36]

Maritole is not the only one to mourn changes in the land. On the walk through Tennessee, Knobowtee notices, "The woods were growing thinner. What would it be without the hills of North Carolina? What would it be without the voices of the trees to help us walk?"[37] In this first section of the walk, with the wooded hills of North Carolina left behind, the land narrative is already being revised. As Maritole spoon-feeds her sister-in-law, Luthy, she tells her, "We've got a new land we're going to. Not the land of North Carolina with yellow leaves. But a new land. The old land won't leave us, Luthy. We carry it within us to wherever we're going."[38] Like the food Maritole feeds to Luthy, the idea of a new land provides sustenance, as does the hope that the "old land won't leave us." These micro land narratives are sustaining narratives for the Trail.

Maritole loses her baby and mother to pneumonia, and she loses the companionship of her husband, who now walks with his brother. Both Maritole and Knobowtee have losses to grieve, but they are unable to comfort each other. A white soldier, Sergeant Williams, makes small gestures toward Maritole, offering her his horse to ride, giving her extra food, dressing her in clothes from the dead (a man's trousers, shirt, and coat) to keep her alive. Where Knobowtee has been emasculated, Maritole has become masculinized on the Trail, both by her clothing and her actions. She responds to Sergeant Williams by telling him a story about the Medicine Lake, "here in this land."[39] Their exchange about where the detachment is at this point—Tennessee or Kentucky— leads to Maritole's reply, "I know, but it's still the same land. Your boundaries don't mean anything to us."[40] Cherokee land exists regardless of state boundaries. Other boundaries are transgressed as well. Her relationship with the white soldier breaches racial and societal boundaries; his act of dressing her in clothes from the dead emphasizes the permeable boundaries between life and death on the Trail. At the same time it blurs gender boundaries, as Maritole wears men's trousers under her dress.

Maritole eventually succumbs to Sergeant Williams's advances, shaming Knobowtee with her transgression. The soldier's attentions do not go unnoticed by the others walking the Trail. Quaty Lewis, whose white husband stayed in North Carolina on her farm, letting Quaty march alone, asks Maritole bitterly, "Is he your husband?" When Maritole replies, "I lost my husband on the trail," Quaty spits, responding, "You agree with the Georgia Cherokee who gave away our land. You deserve the trail."[41] Quaty's response, as Chadwick Allen notes, implicates Maritole, making her complicit with the forces behind the Removal as she moves between "resistance and collaboration."[42] This becomes Maritole and Knobowtee's story of the Trail, from the musket and seed corn left behind in North Carolina, to Knobowtee's inability to comfort Maritole after their baby's death.

The many voices of the novel carry stories with them on the Trail, of Selu; of animals; of Uk'ten, the serpent; of Thunder; but also of the loaves and fishes, told by Reverend Bushyhead; and of the spells and medicines of the conjurers. At one crucial point, Maritole retells the Cherokee creation story to her father, just prior to his death. The retelling of the creation of Elohi during a forced march to a land that no one has yet seen is, for Maritole, a way of keeping the act of creation alive. As Cherokee scholar Jace Weaver explains,

The Cherokee, like other Native peoples, are spatially rather than temporally oriented. Their culture, spirituality, and identity are connected to the land—and not just land in a generalized, fungible sense but *their* land. The act of creation is not so much about what happened *then* as it is what happened *here*. Thus when Indian tribes were forcibly removed from their homes, they were robbed of more than land. Taken from them was a numinous landscape where every mountain and lake held meaning. For example, the Cherokee word *eloh'*, sometimes translated as "religion," also means knowledge, history, culture, law—and land. And it means all these things all the time at the same time. Because of these intimate interrelationships, relocation was an assault upon Native culture, identity, and personhood.[43]

Land, then, is all-encompassing within Cherokee society. Stories are not only *tied* to certain land formations and places, but they form a *part* of the land. When Maritole retells the creation story to her dying father, she is paving the way for him to return home. She is telling the story near the end of the Trail, when the need for a new world is urgent. The retelling also re-creates Cherokee Elohi in all its manifestations on the Trail, easing the way to Indian Territory for some and, for others, easing the way to the world beyond. The act of retelling forms a part of the Trail's land narrative.

Included in this complex concept of knowledge/history/culture/law/ religion/land are stories. "Stories," Knobowtee testifies at one point, "fuel my walk."[44] The Basket Maker, who appears in the text only twice, holds that "the idea for baskets came from our stories. The baskets hold fish and corn and beans. Just like our stories hold meaning."[45] Her pronouncement elicits strong responses:

"You're making that up."
"We need new ways."
"You can't make stories on your own."
"Why not? The trail needs stories."[46]

This discussion between the Basket Maker and the other women is a self-reflexive commentary on the meaning of stories and their role in a newly changing Cherokee society. The declaration that "the trail needs stories" is itself embedded within a Trail story, with all stories layered together and attached to land. The Trail stories mix with the memories of home; Maritole laments, "Nothing would be like the land we came from. Nothing would be like the ceremonies we had there."[47] Maritole's memories of North Carolina become interlinked with her Trail story, in the process forming a new land narrative. By the time the detachment nears Fort Gibson, the end of the Trail, Maritole and Knobowtee have come to some sort of reconciliation, just as the Eastern and Western Cherokees came together under the name of the Cherokee Nation in a July 12, 1839, Act of Union.

Glancy's sequel, *Pushing the Bear: After the Trail of Tears*, takes up the narrative upon the group's arrival in Indian Territory. It is written in the third person; the fragmentation of the Trail is now over. The Cherokee are unaccustomed to the new land, so much so that even "[t]he noise in the new territory was new . . . the stars and moon with their different shapes. There were fewer trees in the new territory, though it also was wooded."[48] Maritole and Knobowtee choose a place to build a cabin and plow a field for corn, "but the soil was a shut door that would not open."[49] Though the land is full of rocks and thick with prairie grasses, a make-shift garden is plowed. In the absence of orators, many of whom were lost to the Trail, Knobowtee "half-prays the seed into the ground," saying, "We're not starting again. We're continuing what our fathers and grandfathers did. It is just in a different place."[50]

This emphasis on "a different place" is repeated throughout the second novel, although there are signs that certain cultural and religious practices, such as the stomp dance, will continue in Indian Territory. The future of other practices, especially those of Cherokee religion, remains unclear. Reverend Bushyhead builds his church and continues his preaching even as the conjurers tell stories and sing bear-hunting songs in the evening. Some Cherokee become Christians in the new territory, while others, like Knobowtee—who comes from a family of conjurers—wrestle with the conflict between honoring their Cherokee religion and adapting to a new one.

Clearly, Indian Territory is not North Carolina. Maritole worries, "Would there be the large snake Uk'ten in the creek with its scales to help the Cherokees? Would there be medicine against the Raven Mocker? . . . Would there be a medicine lake? No, those were the old stories that didn't apply to the new land."[51] Her worries about the "old" stories are undermined by Knobowtee's experience plowing the prairie, which causes him to imagine that Nun'yunu'wi, the stone man, has arrived in the new territory.[52] The novel ends with Maritole and Knobowtee taking a middle path. Maritole becomes a Christian and asks Knobowtee to agree to have their marriage blessed by Reverend Bushyhead. Yet in the final scene, they call a conjurer to help dig a well. Inside the cabin, Maritole is transported through the conjurers' song back to the land she left behind. At the same time, she looks at the dirt on her hands and under her nails, dirt from the new territory. She bids "*[good-bye.] Good-bye. You were all to me. But I give up remembering. Now I help plow the new field. You only get in the way. Move over—*."[53]

In Glancy's recounting of this fictional Trail story, the many losses Maritole has suffered have changed her to the extent that she "give[s] up remembering" the eastern landscape to which she clung so tightly at the beginning of the first novel. But "giv[ing] up remembering" is not the same thing as deliberately forgetting. By telling the metaphorical bear that represents her memories of the Cherokee eastern homelands to "move over," Maritole makes a space for the new land and the new narratives that come with it.

The Long Walk of the Navajo to Hwééldi, or Fort Sumner, in 1864 is as tragic as, but less familiar than, the Cherokee Trail of Tears. In the fall of 1863, Lieutenant Colonel Kit Carson and his troops began a scorched-earth campaign to drive the Navajo from their lands, which are marked by six sacred mountains. Homes, agricultural fields, and orchards were burned to the ground; sheep were slaughtered. Without food or shelter, thousands surrendered, only to be marched some three to five hundred miles to Bosque Redondo in southeastern New Mexico. Approximately nine thousand Navajo and five hundred Mescalero Apache were interned at Fort Sumner, or Hwééldi ("the suffering times" in the Navajo language), for four years, during which they endured tremendous hardship. The U.S. government contemplated relocating the Navajo to a reservation in Oklahoma, but Navajo leader Barboncito argued successfully for a return to Dinetah, the Navajo homeland. The Treaty of Bosque Redondo was signed in June 1868, paving the way for the return home.

Luci Tapahonso's poem "In 1864" and an oral account on YouTube of the Navajo walk to Hwééldi, "Grandma Margaret's Long Walk Story," are but two contemporary examples of land narratives of dispossession.[54] "In 1864" is a multilayered narrative poem that unfurls three different accounts of the Navajo Long Walk to Bosque Redondo. It begins with a framed narrative of a family car trip through New Mexico, with the turnoff to Fort Sumner, the official name of Bosque Redondo, triggering the second story—that of a Navajo man installing power lines in what appears to be Bosque Redondo. Once again, the land triggers stories: "The land was like / he had imagined it from the old stories— flat and dotted with shrubs" (lines 11–12).[55] At night, the land comes alive with "cries and moans carried by the wind / and blowing snow" (18–19). The Navajo man "would turn over and pray / . . . He sang for himself, his family, and the people whose spirits / lingered on the plains, in the arroyos, and in the old windswept plants" (20, 23–24). He leaves the jobsite the next morning, unable to stay in this place-world marked by tragedy, by the "pain and cries of his relatives" (30).

The traveling family stops for food, and the speaker's aunt begins "the story" as she always does, with the words "You are here / because of what happened to your great-grandmother long ago" (33–34). The word "here" refers to Dinetah, Navajo country, to which the Diné finally returned after four years in captivity at Fort Sumner / Bosque Redondo. The story begins as so many other stories of forced removal begin: "They began rounding up the people in the fall" (35). While some hide out in canyons and foothills, others, like the speaker's family, decide to march. The army, led by Carson, has already burned the Navajo fields and slaughtered their sheep, leaving the storyteller to ask, "What would our lives / be like without sheep, crops, and land?" (47–48). This is not a rhetorical question, but one rooted in lived experience. The storyteller links the slaughter of the sheep to the many Diné deaths on the Long Walk—those shot by soldiers for not keeping up with the group, those drowned while crossing the Rio Grande. As the poem's epigraph details, 8,354 Navajo (Diné) were held for four years at Fort Sumner before they were able to return to their homelands. During their captivity, more than 2,500 people died of disease and exposure. Despite the hardships and deprivations, the Diné survived. The storyteller explains:

[W]e told each other, "We will be strong, as long as we are together."
I think that was what kept us alive. We believed in ourselves
and the old stories that the holy people had given us.
"This is why," she would say to us. "This is why we are here.
Because our grandparents prayed and grieved for us." (76–80)

The poem becomes a story of survival and sacrifice for future generations, of relying on the "old stories" and incorporating new ones into the land narrative repertoire. As in *Pushing the Bear*, the land is sustenance during these "suffering times." The poetic frame switches back to the present, as the speaker's daughter cries softly. The speaker tells her "that it was at Bosque Redondo the people learned to use flour" and "it was there that we acquired a deep appreciation for strong coffee" (83, 85). It was also there that what is now considered "traditional" Diné dress—"long, tiered calico skirts / and fine velvet shirts for the men"—was developed (86–87). These "traditional" foods and dress became incorporated into Diné culture. They are reminders of both sacrifice and survivance, and they are part of the land narrative tradition.

In contrast to Tapahonso's poetic rendering, "Grandma Margaret's Long Walk Story" is an open-access social media text. It was uploaded to YouTube on March 3, 2009, by daybreakwarrior, who identifies himself as Grandma Margaret's grandson. There is no other identifying information for Margaret; no last name, community, chapter house, or clan is provided. The video camera focuses on Grandma Margaret, who sits on a couch with a Pendleton blanket draped over the back. She is wearing the "traditional" clothing mentioned in Tapahonso's poem: a velvet blouse and pleated skirt, with a turquoise pin attached to her blouse. Somewhere offscreen, a dog barks, and two young men murmur in agreement from time to time.

Grandma Margaret tells her family's story of the walk to Hwééldi entirely in the Navajo language, with no English translation. I understand only two words—"Hwééldi" and "bilagáana" (non-Diné people)— yet Grandma Margaret's body language suggests that this is a difficult story for her to tell. She rocks her body back and forth slightly; she fidgets, smoothing her hair and touching her right ear. This is an extraordinary oral history, one available to a privileged (Navajo-speaking) audience only. The story thus stays within the community, although it is accessible if one has Internet access. In his notes for the video clip, daybreakwarrior states, "My grandma tells our family's Long Walk story to Hwééldi, Navajo for Fort Sumner. It comes from the Spanish word for Fort, fuerte."[56] As of July 22, 2014, the video has generated 11,014 views and thirty-six comments from speakers of Navajo and non-speakers, Navajo and non-Navajo. Not surprisingly, there are a number of requests for an English translation.

A few of the comments provide insight into Grandma Margaret's oral narrative. Leo Leonard posts, "[A]wesome story my aunt gave. Especially about the Long Walk and for what the lady did for our great-great-grandmother? It makes me wonder if there is a way to honor this lady's Descendants or the people?" Etsosio1 adds, "This is a really powerful story and really does go to prove how important women and the culture are. She talked of how she and all her grandkids are who they are because her grandma strived." This last comment gestures toward Tapahonso's poem, which comes to the same conclusion—thereby linking the two together across the years and the digital divide. Etsosio1's comment also provides a glimpse of gender in action, emphasizing the importance of women in Navajo culture.

A partial understanding of Grandma Margaret's story as a non-Navajo speaker requires listening (to the story), viewing (the storyteller in action), and reading (the online comments that provide clues as to what the story is about). At the same time, the viewer should understand that this is a family story, and it may never be totally accessible to outsiders.

Like the Cherokee Trail of Tears stories, histories of the Long Walk are passed down orally within families and across generations. In the case of Grandma Margaret, they are videotaped, and the videos are uploaded to YouTube for a wider (Navajo-speaking) audience. They appear in collections such as *Oral History Stories of the Long Walk—Hwéeldi Baa Hané*, published by the Navajo Nation in 1990. They are stories of the survival and resurgence of a nation.

In 1991, New Mexico State Monuments, the Museum of New Mexico, and Navajo and Apache leaders began the process of creating a memorial at Bosque Redondo, which lies approximately six miles southeast of the Fort Sumner village. Designed by Diné architect David Sloan, the memorial is in the combined shape of a Diné hogan and an Apache tipi. It contains a museum, a gift shop, and interpretive trails. Construction on phase three of the memorial is underway, as are plans for a new interactive museum display.[57] The mission statement of the Bosque Redondo Memorial is "to respectfully interpret the history of two cultures, the Diné (Navajo) and the N'dé (Mescalero Apache) during the United States government's military campaign of ethnic persecution during the 1860s."[58]

Rather than "shap[e] the public's perception" of the Diné and N'dé past, as Lonetree argues is the role of Native and indigenous museums, it would appear from the Bosque Redondo Memorial's forceful mission statement that its founders and creators are more interested in "shaping the public's perception" of the U.S. military campaigns of the 1860s.[59] And in an ironic twist, while the U.S. Army was responsible for the Long Walk of the Diné and N'dé, it is the U.S. Department of Defense that has been the largest donor of funds to the construction of the memorial.[60] However, the questions remain: Who is this memorial for?

Who will take the time to visit it? As we have seen from "Grandma Margaret's Long Walk Story," the emotional story of the Long Walk is still being passed down within family units. Will Diné and N'dé descendants make the long journey to southeastern New Mexico to see the place where their relatives were forcibly interned? Or are this story and this memorial for a different group of descendants?

CHAPTER TWO

"This Scrap of Earth"

Louise Erdrich, Environmentalism, and the Postallotment Reservation

This ain't real estate.

—LOUISE ERDRICH, *The Bingo Palace*

In the end, of course, it all comes back to the land.

—LOUISE ERDRICH AND MICHAEL DORRIS,
"Who Owns the Land?"

. . . the scraps told our story.

—LOUISE ERDRICH, *Tracks*

IMPLICITLY OR EXPLICITLY, LOUISE ERDRICH'S body of work holds Anishinaabe land and its multilayered narratives at its center.[1] These land narratives take a variety of forms, but all foreground the contrapuntal subtext of Anishinaabe—and all Indian—land: dispossession. Erdrich's travel narrative, the aptly titled *Books and Islands in Ojibwe Country* (2003), opens with a map depicting the "Ojibwe Country" of Erdrich's journey from Minneapolis, Minnesota, to the "book-islands" of the Lake of the Woods, which straddle the U.S.-Canadian border—all, incidentally, Ojibwe land at one time.[2] The words "Ojibwe Country" appear in boldfaced print in the upper-right corner of the rectangular map. "Ontario" and "Minnesota," both Indian place-names, are displayed

45

prominently, along with the names of U.S. and Canadian Ojibwe reservations, reserves, and on-reservation communities. The names of the United States and Canada appear only in the insets of North America and the Red Lake Reservation in the bottom-right and top-left corners of the map. With their miniscule type, they recede from the map, centering "Ojibwe Country" within the context of cartographic representation. Erdrich's travel narrative and accompanying map, published by the National Geographic Society as part of its Literary Travel Series, depict only twenty-first-century Ojibwe land holdings in Minnesota and Ontario. The reader is positioned to imagine—or, alternatively, to ignore—the vast expanse of the original "Ojibwe Country," which stretched both north and south from the border, separating the United States and Canada, from the eastern woodlands to the Great Lakes and beyond. What the depiction of this contemporary "Ojibwe Country" map leaves us with are the ishkoniganan: the reservations, or, in contemporary Anishinaabemowin, the leftovers.[3]

How these reservations ostensibly set aside for the Anishinaabeg came to be viewed as "leftovers" is a long and complicated story, one to which justice cannot be done in a single telling (or a single hearing). Yet these reservations, or leftovers, form part of the land narratives Erdrich spins while relating the stories of the inhabitants of the fictional reservation Little No Horse, its three border towns, and their relationship to the land they live with. In examining these narratives, it is useful to consider the Anishinaabe word for map, "akii-mazina'igaan." Consisting of two words, "akii," or land, and "mazina'igaan," or book, paper, or document, the term literally means "land book." It invites us to read the land, and the narratives it holds, as texts.

Erdrich's textual land narratives tell the story of the ishkonigan, of what is left over, of the messy business of land tenure in Indian Country and its close relative, land dispossession. Like the forced removals discussed in chapter 1, which remain defining moments in the Cherokee and Navajo tribal histories, the General Allotment Act of 1887 (also called the Dawes Act) wields considerable influence to this day in defining the Anishinaabe postallotment reservation landscape. Land lost through tax liens and forfeitures, and made "surplus" in turn, became checkerboard reservations. Trust land lies next to land in fee-simple title; Indian neighbors reside next to non-Indian neighbors; jurisdiction changes from one side of the street to the other. Former Anishinaabe fishing camps, which in turn became part of Native allotments along lakeshores, are now tourist lodges for city fishermen.

This chapter considers the terrain of these constantly shifting reservation landscapes in relation to Louise Erdrich's interlinked series of novels set on a fictional North Dakota reservation, Little No Horse: *Love Medicine* (1984), *Tracks* (1988), *The Beet Queen* (1986), *The Bingo Palace* (1994), *The Last Report on the Miracles at Little No Horse* (2001), and *Four Souls* (2004). When read in narrative sequence, beginning with *Tracks* (1988), these novels define the stakes involved for Native people living in the contested spaces of the postallotment reservation, stakes that appear to be invisible to the larger non-Native population. By using the term "postallotment," I mean to show that the dispossession and alienation of Native land resulting from allotment in severalty are part of an ongoing process, one that did not abruptly come to an end in 1934 with the passage of the Indian Reorganization Act. Rather, it reaches both backward and forward through time, up to the present day.[4] Even before the Allotment Act was made into law, allotment in severalty formed part of a number of treaties negotiated with tribal nations during the nineteenth century, often twinned with offers of citizenship. It continues on in the form of fractionated heirships, mismanaged trust lands, and Individual Indian Money (IIM) accounts, as the *Cobell* lawsuit discussed in the introduction demonstrated. Further, dispossession on the postallotment reservation is not only a land tenure issue, but it is intimately linked with environmental issues as well. The generic legal language of allotment reveals the Anglo-American legislative histories of reservation lands, yet at the same time, that language masks realities—of the loss of land, and of what the land represents culturally, environmentally, economically, and politically to Native people.

Land and the people's relation to it are at the heart of Erdrich's North Dakota series of novels. "Land," as Jace Weaver notes, "is an ordinate category for Native peoples."[5] The Ojibwe still retain the memory of their migration from the east to their present homelands in the Great Lakes area and the northern plains of North Dakota and Montana.[6] This migration narrative is carried over into Erdrich's novel *Tracks*, in which the character of Fleur Pillager figures prominently. *Tracks* and its sequel, *Four Souls* (2004), follow Fleur as she struggles to hold on to her land, loses it to tax forfeiture, then reclaims it, deforested, all at great personal loss. By tracking Fleur and her land narrative through Erdrich's novels, we see the effects of allotment in severalty from both a land tenure and environmental perspective. While there is no mention of the Allotment Act in either *Tracks* or *Four Souls*, its repercussions are on every page; they also spill over into the other interlinked novels that make up the sequence of narratives set on and around Little No Horse.[7] In *Love Medicine* (1984), set some sixty years later, Albertine describes the continuing effects of allotment, which she experienced while growing up with her mother on the reservation. They lived

> in an aqua-and-silver trailer, set next to the old house on the land where my great-grandparents were allotted when the government decided to turn Indians into farmers. The policy of allotment was a joke. As I was driving toward the land, looking around, I saw as usual how much of the reservation was sold to whites and lost forever.[8]

Albertine describes allotment as a "policy" rather than a legislative act, but she concisely sums up the intent: to transform each Native man into the supposed ideal man of the assimilation era, a farmer. What matters here is not necessarily the legislative act itself, but the effects of land dispossession on subsequent generations.[9] Albertine's sense of land "lost forever" echoes the sentiments of many Native people during the 1970s and 1980s, when Erdrich was writing her first three published novels. It was a time of activism, both on and off the reservation and in the courts of law. The American Indian Movement (AIM) began in Minneapolis in 1968 as a response to local police brutality, but quickly gained a national stage for pan-Indian concerns, including land tenure issues such as termination. The 1970s also saw the pan-Indian takeover of Alcatraz Island in San Francisco Bay, the siege at Wounded Knee on the Pine Ridge Reservation in South Dakota, and the march on Washington, D.C., to publicize the Trail of Broken Treaties. All received national media coverage. This period also saw the conclusion of the termination era, which sought to end the sovereign status of Indian tribes, and the beginning of a new era of tribal land reclamation efforts to reverse the losses of allotment.

It was in the middle of this flurry of Indian activism that Erdrich wrote her first two novels and the four-hundred-page manuscript that would become *Tracks*.[10] While Erdrich's work has undergone an appraisal in recent years in terms of its political content, in 1986 she was taken to task by fellow writer Leslie Marmon Silko for her alleged "self-referential writing" into which "no history or politics intrudes."[11] That particular criticism was leveled at Erdrich's second novel, *The Beet Queen*, which takes place in the fictional reservation border town of Argus. The same criticism cannot be leveled at Erdrich's subsequent novels—especially *Tracks*, which was shaped into its current form during a period of illegal land conveyances on the White Earth Reservation and five other member reservations of the Minnesota Chippewa Tribe.

In the 1960s, the county of Clearwater, Minnesota, illegally placed an eighty-acre trust allotment of land belonging to Zay Zah, a tribal member from the White Earth Reservation, onto the county tax rolls, then subsequently turned it over to the state for unpaid taxes. The parcel was eventually put up for public sale. This activity came to light when the purchasers filed for quiet title, and Zay Zah's grandson and sole heir, George Aubid Sr., filed an action in state court, challenging the county's actions. The court's 1978 finding in favor of Aubid led to an investigation of land tenure statuses on the state's Chippewa reservations. According to Holly Youngbear-Tibbetts, "The investigation uncovered a multitude of illegal and unauthorized title conveyances dating as far back as the 1905 allotment of treaty lands and as recently as the 1960s."[12] This in turn resulted in the clouding of hundreds of land titles, pitting heirs of allottees against non-Indian landowners on the checkerboard White Earth Reservation, similarly to the way in which the "holdouts" are pitted against the "sellers" to the lumber companies in *Tracks*.

In September 1988, just as *Tracks* was about to be published, Erdrich and her then husband Michael Dorris wrote a feature article in the *New York Times Magazine* tracing the Zay Zah case back to the Allotment Act. They visited the White Earth Reservation and surrounding communities to speak with members of two grassroots organizations, Anishinaabe-akii (The People's Land) and the United Township, made up of non-Indian landowners.[13] Far from merely reading up on the political struggles over land at White Earth, Erdrich immersed herself in them. The timing of the publication of the article in a national news source alongside the novel's publication was undoubtedly a marketing move; nevertheless, the two works illuminate one another in terms of their historical and political contexts.[14] Similarly, the Zay Zah case illuminates the simultaneous vernacular and official landscapes of the postallotment reservation, demonstrating that land tenure is still an issue some eighty years after the Allotment Act was officially ended. To understand how this is possible, let us turn now to a brief history of the workings of the act.

The road to the General Allotment Act of 1887 was long and complicated, as the catalog of the disastrous effects of the act continues to be. By the time Senator Henry Dawes of Massachusetts introduced his severalty bill to Congress in February 1886, the topic had been a matter of discussion in many circles for some time. As Wilcomb E. Washburn has shown, the doctrine of allotment in severalty was not a new development, having been made part of a number of treaties during the first half of the nineteenth century.[15] While Dawes is linked by name to the Allotment Act, he was not the first to introduce a severalty bill before Congress. That honor went to Senator Richard Coke of Texas, who introduced two separate severalty bills in 1881 and 1884, neither of which passed. Dawes himself was up to his elbows in matters of Indian policy and affairs; he was instrumental in attaching an amendment to a standard appropriations bill for the benefit of the Yankton Sioux in 1871, essentially ending the Indian treaty-making system in the United States. Records of congressional debates from this period reveal Dawes's underlying intent to end the treaty system as a first step toward allotment of Indian lands.[16]

The push for allotment came from both politicians and civilian reformist groups, who were united by a common belief that the individual ownership of land and "civilization" went hand in hand. The Board of Indian Commissioners, established by an act of Congress in 1869, repeatedly recommended "the divisions of lands now held in common, and the endowment of each Indian family with a *permanent* home" in its annual reports (emphasis mine).[17] Similarly, the main objectives of the Women's National Indian Association, the Indian Rights Association, and the Lake Mohonk Conference of the Friends of the Indians focused on the "civilizing" aim of allotment in severalty. Despite the large number of supporters of allotment, there were public figures in opposition, including politicians. Representative Russel Errett of Pennsylvania spoke for the minority on the Committee on Indian Affairs in its 1880 report, stating, "The real aim of this bill is to get at the Indian lands and open them up to settlement."[18]

According to the Allotment Act, land was allotted "to each head of a family" in the amount of 160 acres, with smaller allotments for single persons, orphaned children, and children under the age of eighteen. The land remaining after allotment was declared "surplus" and opened up for white settlement, realizing Representative Errett's prediction of 1880. Individual allotments were to be held in trust for twenty-five years, a period that was shortened by a series of offshoot laws, both on the federal (the Burke Act of 1906) and state (Minnesota's Steenerson Act of 1904 and Clapp Rider of 1906) levels, further opening up Native lands for sale to homesteaders, speculators, and lumber interests. The Burke Act did away with the trust period entirely for those Indians deemed competent, paving the way for families to sell allotments or lose them to tax liens. Under the Steenerson Act, heads of households on the

White Earth Reservation received an additional eighty acres of land, with no restrictions on timber sales. Congressman Moses E. Clapp, formerly a local attorney for the lumber cartels, authored a rider to the Indian Appropriations Act of 1906 that lifted all restrictions on the sale, taxation, and mortgage of a mixed-blood member's past or future trust land at White Earth upon the individual's request.[19] These pieces of legislation, in concert with the General Allotment Act, would change the landscape of Ojibwe Country forever.

By all measures, the General Allotment Act failed to achieve its assimilative mission. What the act and its subsequent amendments did accomplish is documented in the government's own records: they caused the loss of ninety million acres of Indian land, representing two-thirds of reservation land.[20] The Allotment Act also radically transformed Native peoples' relationships with both the land and their own social and kinship systems by replacing a communal land base with individually held parcels. The authors and agents of the act essentially rewrote the narrative between the Anishinaabeg and their land.

Tracks opens in the winter of 1912, amid "a new sickness . . . [called] the consumption" that will take the lives of many reservation community members, yet will spare the three main characters: the tribal elder Nanapush; Pauline Puyat, a young mixed-race Chippewa woman who leaves the reservation for the border town of Argus; and Fleur Pillager, the only member of her family to survive.[21] All three become dispossessed in a number of ways. The consumption is not the only form of devastation to sweep through the reservation that year; 1912 also marked the first year during which Indian land allotted under the General Allotment Act could be sold.[22] The novel comes to an end in the spring of 1924, the year that saw the passage of the Indian Citizenship Act. The novel is thus set firmly within the purview of federal Indian law, drawing attention to the ways such law sets the parameters for, and intrudes on, numerous aspects of daily Indian life.

The narrative action pivots around Fleur Pillager and her allotment land on the shores of Lake Matchimanito, where Misshepeshu, the

Great Lynx, is said to live. Many of the novel's crucial moments take place there, among them Fleur's "return" from a nearly fatal bout of consumption, her three near deaths by drowning, and her figurative environmental "death" from the clear-cutting of the forest surrounding her cabin. Throughout *Tracks*, Fleur is poised between life and death, possession and dispossession, a balance represented by the novel's alternating narrators. Tribal elder Nanapush and Pauline Puyat provide point and counterpoint narration of Fleur's story of dispossession: they describe her parents and siblings; her daughter, Lulu; her born-too-soon son; her perceived powers; her land; and her access to both what the land holds and what it signifies for her. Though other characters are also dispossessed, it is Fleur—described by Nanapush as "the funnel of our history"—who is depicted as most fully living the experiences of dispossession and environmental degradation.[23]

Nanapush counters dispossession through the careful conservation of his tribal name—and, by extension, through his Anishinaabe identity, through resistance to being put on government lists. His name, he tells Lulu, is one "that loses power every time it is written and stored in a government file. That is why I only gave it out once in all those years."[24] The power of his name derives from its association with Nanaboozhoo, the Anishinaabe culture hero of traditional stories. He was given the name by his father, "because it's got to do with trickery and living in the bush . . . [t]he first Nanapush stole fire. You will steal hearts." With his Jesuit education, Nanapush "could have written [his] name . . . in script," but instead he chooses to give out "*No Name*" to the church missionaries and Indian agents for their censuses and tribal rolls.[25] On the one occasion when Nanapush does give out his tribal name, for Lulu's church baptismal certificate, he does so on what turns out to be the official document that has the power to bring Lulu home from government school.

In contrast, Pauline has a history of dispossession, which begins long before the narrative starts. She is a Puyat, who are "mixed-bloods, skinners in the clan for which the name was lost." In a tribal context, she is of low social standing; in Argus, she is so "poor looking" that she is invisible to customers and laborers at the butcher shop where she works.[26] "The skinners," as Nanapush calls the Puyats when recounting his tale to Lulu, are "always an uncertain people, shy, never leaders in our dances and cures."[27] According to Nanapush, Pauline herself was "an unknown mixture of ingredients, like pale bannock that sagged or hardened. We never knew what to call her, or where she fit or how to think when she was around."[28] Just as Fleur is the "last Pillager," Pauline is the last Puyat on the reservation, "the only trace of those who died and scattered."[29] They are in opposition to each other: one has been dispossessed by the processes of colonialism begun long before allotment, and the other is just beginning the journey of postallotment dispossession. Fleur gives birth to children, while Pauline dispossesses the reservation of its souls—like that of Mary Pepewas, whose sickbed Pauline attends to—dispatching them to Christ. Upon hearing no word from her family after the consumption epidemic sweeps the reservation, Pauline dreams of her sisters and mother swaying in the tree branches, part of a traditional burial practice discouraged by the priests. In her dream, the bodies of her sisters and mother, which were "dragged down[,] had *no names* to them" (emphasis mine).[30] In a sense, both Nanapush and Pauline are nameless, the former by choice and the latter by circumstances. Both are dispossessed. When Nanapush loses his allotment to back taxes, he moves to Kashpaw land, forming a new family with Margaret and Lulu. Pauline, in contrast, is left alone and rootless in Argus after her family disappears from the reservation, either because of consumption or because they have fled north. She seeks shelter with others—first with Bernadette Morrissey and then at a convent on the hill. Nanapush manages to salvage his name and his Anishinaabe identity, whereas Pauline leaves her Puyat lineage, such as it is, behind, adopting a new name, Leopolda, and a new identity as a Catholic nun.

Everyone has something to say about Fleur Pillager except, of course, Fleur herself. She remains an enigma, as ephemeral as the sea foam on the rocky shore of Lake Matchimanito, yet in a strange way she is as tangible as the land itself. Schooled in the old ways, in what today would be referred to in certain circles as "traditional ecological knowledge,"

Fleur is a holdout from previous generations and centuries. Her story crosses generations, even as it crosses the various novels in Erdrich's North Dakota series. Fleur's identification with land is a constant, from her activities of daily living to the community stories about her hunting prowess—and to her relationship with Misshepeshu, the lake man. Her relationship with Misshepeshu arises in Pauline's beginning narrative, which is resonant with community stories about Fleur's first two drownings; "the death a Chippewa cannot survive."[31] Precisely because Fleur did survive, "nobody dares to court her," say the community gossips, as "it was clear that Misshepeshu, the water man, the monster, wanted her for himself."[32] Misshepeshu forms a part of the Pillager vernacular landscape, in which land is not "ordinary land to buy and sell."[33] The lake man has his own story of dispossession, having followed the Pillagers after they were "driven from the east." While the Anishinaabe community understands the Pillager landscape, with its death roads and fresh graves from the consumption epidemic, outsiders do not. They trespass at their own risk.

The dispossession and environmental devastation of Fleur's land is foreshadowed from the beginning of the novel. In the first chapter, set in the winter of 1912, Nanapush tells Fleur's daughter, Lulu,

> My girl, I saw the passing of times you will never know. I guided the last buffalo hunt. I saw the last bear shot. I trapped the last beaver with a pelt of more than two years' growth. I spoke aloud the words of the government treaty, and refused to sign the settlement papers that would take away our woods and lake. I axed the last birch thatwas older than I, and I saved the last Pillager.[34]

Nanapush's catalog of the "last," whether the last buffalo or birch tree, speaks to the environmental devastation wrought by the fur trade, the forced removals westward after the signing of treaties, the reservation system, and the Allotment Act and other legislation. The destruction has spread out across temporal scales, gradually revealing itself—as did the consumption that wiped out half the tribe, which was "different from the pox and fever, for it came on slow."[35] The last Pillager, of course, is Fleur, who, like the land, endures the hardships of dispossession and environmental devastation. After Nanapush finds Fleur barely alive in the Pillager cabin, he bundles her onto a sled, takes her home, and nurses her back to health. By spring, Fleur has returned to her family allotment at Matchimanito, despite Nanapush's pleas for her to stay and his insistences that "the land will be sold and measured."[36] Nanapush relates:

> I watched the wagons take the rutted turnoff to Matchimanito. Few of them returned, it is true, but those that did were enough, loaded high with hard green wood. From where we now sit, granddaughter, I heard the groan and crack, felt the ground tremble as each tree slammed earth. I weakened into an old man as one oak went down, another and another was lost, as a gap formed here, a clearing there, and plain daylight entered.[37]

What Nanapush describes is the Allotment Act in action—he depicts the measuring and sale of land, the extraction of its resources, and the effects of those actions on the novel's characters. Fleur's perceived powers have already begun to fail her: "Her dreams lied, her vision was obscured, her helper slept deep in the lake."[38] Throughout *Tracks*, trees in all their possible permutations function as a metaphor for the Anishinaabeg, individually and collectively. As the deforestation of the land surrounding Matchimanito begins—slowly at first, one tree at a time, the valuable oaks the first to go, eventually creating artificial clearings in the deep woods—so do the divisions in the reservation community, over the issue of land sales to the lumber cartels.

> *We watched as Damien unfolded and smoothed the map flat on the table. In the dizzying smell of coffee roasting, of bannock cooking, we examined the lines and circles of the homesteads paid up—Morrissey, Pukwan, Hat, Lazarres everywhere. They were colored green. The lands that were gone out of the tribe—the deaths with no heirs, to sales, to the lumber company—were painted a pale and rotten pink. Those in*

question, a sharper yellow. At the center of a bright square was
Matchimanito, a small blue triangle I could cover with my hand.[39]

In the quote above, the focal point is yet another map, this one representing ishkonigan, or reservation, land allotments in various stages of
possession ("homesteads paid up") and dispossession—those lost to
foreclosures, distress sales, sales by deceit or undue persuasion, and
intestate proceedings.[40] Then there are those "homesteads" in the most
precarious state of all: in arrears on annual taxes. Neither "paid up" nor
"foreclosed" on, these allotments are, like their fictional owners, in a
state of flux, caught between competing discourses on land, law, and the
natural environment. Color-coded by legal status, the "lines and circles"
on the map, which represent homesteads and allotments, reflect the
material presence of the General Allotment Act of 1887.[41] Allotment, as
G. Thomas Couser has noted, "is crucial to the internal politics of the
novel," highlighting as it does the emerging factionalism of clans and
families within the tribe, who do not agree about entering into arrange-
ments with government agents and lumber companies eager to harvest
the reservation's vast stands of timber.[42] Just as crucial are the land narratives contained within *Tracks*, represented only in part by the Indian
agent's map: those of the topography of Anishinaabe land, with its deep
bush, wooded forests, clearings, and the lake, Matchimanito, that is, the
spiritual and cultural nexus of the community. Against a domestic
backdrop of coffee roasting and bread baking, the land itself is reduced
to color-coded symbols delineating where dispossession begins and
ends, and where access to natural resources and culturally and spiritu-
ally important sites is cut off.

The subjects of the quote above, the extended family of Fleur,
Nanapush, Margaret, and Margaret's sons, Eli and Nector, will similarly
have their access cut off in the form of surveyor lines and flags, plat lines,
fences, telegraph poles, and other markers of the so-called progress
imposed by the act. It is here, in the contested terrain of the postallotment
reservation, where the discourses of land, law, and natural environment
clash, their consequences playing out on a local stage as well as a national

one. For the Anishinaabeg of Erdrich's novels—and for all Indian communities in the United States—these triple discourses are inextricably entwined. From the very beginning of Indian-settler relations, prime agricultural land, grazing land, access to waterways, and old-growth timber were all part of the high-stakes negotiations that made up the treaty system. Following that system's demise in 1871, these all informed the smooth moves of the processes of federal Indian law. Although treaties could no longer be used as negotiating tools for Indian land, federal legislation could use civilizing rhetoric as a cover for land grabs.

As the extended family examines the Indian agent's map, Nanapush takes careful note of the "lapping pink" squares demarcating "land we would never walk or hunt, from which our children would be barred."[43] His use of the communal "we" reflects the Allotment Act's purpose: to do away with communally owned tribal land and move toward a system of individually owned plots, while opening up any surplus land for sale to non-Indian homesteaders. This "barr[ing]" of future generations from land means not only the loss of access to land, but it also denies access to the very things the land produces: small game; bushes, brambles, and trees bearing fruit, nuts, and berries; birch bark for canoes, baskets, and shelter; medicinal plants; reeds, cattails, and other aquatic plants used for baskets and woven mats; stands of wild rice; fish; and water. The triangular tract includes Lake Matchimanito, home to fish and other water animals, relatives to the Ojibwe through the Ojibwe dodems, or clans. In other words, almost everything the people will need and depend upon for the future lies within the boundaries of soon-to-be dispossessed tracts. Allotment in severalty was, as White Earth scholar Lawrence Gross declares, "the end of the world as the Anishinaabeg had known it."[44]

Nanapush also comes to this realization, arguing with Father Damien, the local priest, "As you know, I was taught by the Jesuits. I know about law. I know that 'trust' means they can't tax our parcels."[45] Nanapush is right, of course, but he can't have anticipated the entanglement between senators, congressmen, Indian agents, and the timber industry, especially with regard to the White Earth Ojibwe in Minnesota and the Turtle Mountain Chippewa in North Dakota, whose histories Erdrich draws upon for the foregrounding of *Tracks*.[46] For Fleur, the Indian agent's map has "no bearing or sense, as no one would be reckless enough to try collecting for land where Pillagers were buried."[47] Thus there are two competing landscapes—and two competing land narratives—at stake in this passage: the vernacular landscape of the Anishinaabe reservation community, with its modest dwellings, hunting and gathering grounds, and sacred sites; and the official landscape represented by the Indian agent's map, an "official" government document. There is the narrative of "trust land" told by the government, ever prone to change as politicians and others holding government appointments rotate in and out, during election cycles in which the Anishinaabeg have no say. The Anishinaabe land narrative includes the subtext of Misshepeshu, who followed Old Man Pillager west to Lake Matchimanito. Too, it includes Fleur's deep knowledge of the natural world, as evidenced by her hunting prowess and her lean-to filled with birch bark boxes of herbs, bark, and bundles of roots for curing. Misshepeshu, in particular, also exists outside Erdrich's textual world. His representations can be found in petroglyphs at Lake Superior Provincial Park in Ontario, on woven mats used for covering traditional dwellings, and on copper discs. His own stories are legion.[48]

Despite Nanapush's protestations, his own allotment and those of the Kashpaws and Fleur are all poised for tax forfeitures. Clued in by Father Damien, the reservation priest, the makeshift clan harvests high-bush cranberry bark to sell to the local dealer for the popular Lydia E. Pinkham tonic, stripping the bushes around Fleur's allotment and into the woods. The smell of the bark on their skin and clothes is "the odor of both salvation and betrayal," as they overharvest the bushes for a chance to save their land.[49] Money is gathered to pay the back taxes, but the final betrayal comes when illegal fines are added onto the total. There is only enough for the Kashpaw allotment. The betrayal is heightened twice more: the Indian agent posted in the area for the protection of the tribe adds on illegal late fees, and Margaret and Nector, in an act of self-preservation, pay on their own allotment at the expense of Fleur and Nanapush. Just as Nanapush describes land as the "only thing that lasts life to life," Fleur describes Margaret's salvation and betrayal in terms of land: "She saved my life twice and now she's taken it back twice . . . [b]ut I will never go to Kashpaw land."[50]

Thus begins the dispossession and deforestation of the Pillager land, and with it, that of the Little No Horse Reservation. Nanapush describes "twisted stumps of trees and scrub, the small, new thriving grasses which had been previously shaded . . . the ugliness, the scraped and raw places, the scattered bits of wood and dust."[51] The reservation roads are crisscrossed by the wheels of heavy lumber wagons, cutting open the earth. As the lumberjacks descend upon Fleur's cabin, Nanapush notices "a forest . . . suspended, lightly held. . . . Nothing was solid. Each green crown was held in the air by no more than splinters of bark. Each tree was sawed through at the base."[52] What Nanapush senses is both the tenuousness of Anishinaabeg survival in the fall of 1919—the forest with its green crowns standing in for the Anishinaabeg—and Fleur's last act before leaving the reservation with her Red River cart piled with moss-wrapped stones, bundles of roots, and the grave markers of her ancestors. Looking back from the safe distance provided by the passage of years, Nanapush recalls in *Four Souls*, "We were snared in laws then. Pitfalls and loopholes. Attempting to keep what was left of our land was like walking through a landscape of webs. With a flare of ink down in the capital city, rights were taken and given."[53] He uses the language of hunting alongside legal terminology to explain the terrain of the postallotment reservation, even as "land dwindled until there wasn't enough to call a hunting territory."[54] In Erdrich's sequence of novels, and as evidenced by both Native and non-Native historical records, non-Natives—such as lumber barons and land speculators— exploit "loopholes" to their own benefit. For the Anishinaabeg, every step is a potential pitfall, every footfall a snare.

The narrative of Fleur's allotment does not end with the deforestation of her land. While *Tracks* tells a narrative of dispossession and deforestation, *Four Souls* holds out the possibilities of land reclamation and a return to a subsistence lifestyle. In *The Last Report on the Miracles at Little No Horse*, a subsequent novel, Father Damien notes in his day-book in 1912 that one John James Mauser has made his way westward as a land speculator, following first the railroad and now the lumber. He is complicit in the Allotment Act and its various amendments, buying "land by having the Ojibwe owners declared incompetent. . . . He takes the trees off. He leaves the stumps."[55] Nanapush's indictment of Mauser in *Four Souls* is even stronger—he accuses Mauser of marrying "young Ojibwe girls straight out of boarding school, applying for their permits to log off the allotment lands they had inherited," and leaving tree stumps and babies behind as he moves on to the next young girl.[56] Further, Mauser seems to be targeting Fleur's allotment. Father Damien observes of Mauser, "He denudes all holdings as they come his way, though sometimes he waits for certain special parcels that produce, as do one series of prime allotments on Little No Horse, oak trees of great density, beauty, and age that will never again be seen in this region."[57]

In a mirroring of the conspiracies surrounding the government offi-cials and lumber barons who deforested the White Earth Reservation, the site of the most egregious violations of the principles of trust and law, Tatro, the Indian agent at Little No Horse, "won a personal commis-sion for discovering that due to a recent government decision the land upon which those trees grew was tax forfeit from one Indian, just a woman—she could go elsewhere and, anyway, she was a trouble-maker."[58] This Indian woman is, of course, Fleur, and she does go else-where, following the trail of the trees. Just as Mauser waited for Fleur's land to come up for auction on unpaid taxes, so does Fleur wait for her chance to avenge the figurative rape of her land. As a cover, she finds employment as a domestic servant at Mauser's home. When she finds Mauser paralyzed, she works to heal him with her traditional cures because, in the words of Nanapush, "she wanted the man healthy so that she could destroy him fresh."[59]

The site of Mauser's mansion in Minneapolis, built with quartersawn oak from Fleur's allotment and brownstone from "an island in the deep cold northern lake called gichi gami"—now also stripped of its trees—was one of importance to the Anishinaabe in earlier times.[60] "The ridge of earth was massive," according to Nanapush; it was a preferred location for spotting enemies or storms and, because of its proximity to water and game, for making camp.[61] In contrast, Polly, Mauser's sister-in-law and a foil to Nanapush, describes the house as situated "on the most exclusive ridge of the city . . . unshadowed yet by trees."[62] The now-denuded ridge, it seems, is still a prime spot for making camp.

Like the Ojibwe woman who gave birth on this spot to a son named Mountain, her spilled blood becoming chokecherries before "the people moved on, pushed west" ahead of the settlers, immigrants, too, give of their blood and sweat, in order to build Mauser's house.[63] The animals living in the city similarly give of their lives—a hundred sandhill cranes are shot down and roasted; a lynx is turned into a spotted muff for Mauser's wife, with one claw to be hung off Mauser's watch fob. Mauser's mansion, however, is anything but a home-place. With a brownstone façade quarried and "hand-cut by homesick Italians"; windows dressed in fine lace from Indian missions; chimneys made of "brick requiring the addition of blood"; and the iron for the keys, locks, and railings mined from the Mesabi Range by Norwegians and Sammi "so gutshot with hunger they didn't care if they were trespassing on anybody's hunting ground or not," Mauser's mansion could be nothing other than a human and environmental disaster.[64]

In this house built with the sweat and labor of immigrants and mission Indians, and with timber from her own allotment land, Fleur's plan for vengeance takes an unexpected turn. She snares Mauser, but instead of dispatching him with her skinning knife, she marries him. After a difficult pregnancy treated with spoonfuls of whiskey, she bears a son, a child who does not speak, who constantly craves sweets, yet who becomes a cardsharp. Mauser's empire crashes like the trees that "crack off and fall away" around Fleur's cabin, but not before he flees from his creditors.[65] Fleur and her son take the automobile, a Pierce-Arrow, and make for the back roads to the reservation, the deed to her land firmly in hand. Once again, there is betrayal—Mauser has failed to pay taxes on the land, and the Indian agent, Tatro, has purchased it from the state during a loophole year. Fleur's deed is worthless. She must develop a new strategy to reclaim her land.

Fleur carefully sets a snare for Tatro, using the Pierce-Arrow as bait. In contrast to the gambling scenes in the butcher shop in *Tracks*, during which Fleur is careful to win exactly one dollar every night to reel in her victims, here she strategically loses to Tatro while feigning inebriation, until she has nothing left but the car. "I ain't steady enough," she informs the crowd that has gathered around. "I'm gonna give my hand over to n'gozis."[66] As Fleur and her son change places, Tatro is confident of a win, unaware that he has been caught in her trap. He puts up the 160-acre parcel on the lake, now deforested, and the island. Once the boy begins to cut the cards deftly, Tatro realizes he never had a chance.

For Tatro, the now-deforested parcel of land is useless, its natural resources exploited and depleted, and it is equal in value to a new model Pierce-Arrow. In other words, the land is a commodity to be sold or traded. In comparison, Fleur's relationship to this parcel of Anishinaabewakii, this Indian land, is as to a relative, with all the duties and obligations that come with such a relationship. In order to be worthy of the land, Fleur must undergo a ritual of return that involves the medicine dress Margaret has made and a new name: Four Souls. (For Fleur, the Pierce-Arrow is simply a means of transportation home and a way to snare Tatro.)

This gambling scene plays out twice across Erdrich's texts, first in *The Bingo Palace* (1994) in an abbreviated form, and in more detail in *Four Souls* (2004). The end result is the same: the reclamation of Fleur's land from Jewett Tatro. Living alone on her allotment land in contemporary times in *The Bingo Palace*, Fleur is still estranged from her grown daughter Lulu, and she is referred to by the community as Mindemoya, or Old Lady. Her descendants, Lipsha Morrisey and Lyman Lamartine, relatives to each other in a complicated way, are at odds over a woman and the economic development of the reservation. Lyman dreams of Fleur repeating, in her bear rasp of a voice, Nanapush's words from *Tracks*: "Land is the only thing that lasts from life to life. Money burns like tinder, flows off like water, and as for the government's promises, the wind is steadier." This is followed by, "This time, don't sell out for a barrel of weevil-shot flour and a mossy pork."[67] Lyman, who has already "carved up the reservation," plans to acquire land to place into trust and build a resort on Fleur's lakefront property, essentially dispossessing her once again.[68] In contrast, Lipsha's vision quest ends with the words "[t]his ain't real estate," spoken by a skunk, echoing Nanapush's earlier sentiments about Pillager land.[69] The new generation on Little No Horse continues its divisions over land and what land represents—but this time those divisions are taking place in a twentieth-century context, following the advent of the gaming industry.

Lipsha is seemingly the spiritual and cultural heir of Fleur, who tells him, "If you're a Pillager then claim so. Don't say Morrissey."[70] Lyman, in contrast, is intently focused on the business end of things; he sees land as something that can be leveraged to make more money. Lipsha describes Lyman's plan to build a casino on land that is "partly Fleur's" and

> partly old allotments that the tribe holds in common, and which is fractionated through the dead and scattered holdouts who have never signed the treaties that gave away so much of what we called ours. Where Fleur's cabin stands, a parking lot will be rolled out of asphalt. Over Pillager grave markers, sawed by wind and softened, blackjack tables. . . . Out upon the lake that the lion man inhabits, where Pillagers drowned and lived, where black stones still roll round to the surface, the great gaming room will face with picture windows.[71]

In this vivid description, Lipsha begins the work of claiming his Pillager ancestry by means of the vernacular landscape that contains Fleur's cabin, the grave markers of Pillager ancestors, and the lake, home of Misshepeshu. This landscape also holds the presence of other, unnamed Anishinaabeg, "the dead and scattered holdouts" who refused to sign the treaties that would give away their land. The fractionated allotments are signposts that point backward in time to the so-called assimilation era and the Allotment Act. They are tangible reminders of the continuing difficulty of land tenure in Ojibwe Country. Both Lipsha and Lyman imagine a future for their Anishinaabe community; any such future bears consequences that cannot yet be revealed. Erdrich ends this dilemma on an ambiguous note—the land narrative will be rewritten, but how? Will Fleur's chances run out? Will she be dispossessed by her great-grandson? Will her card games give way to blackjack tables? Will money win out over land? What happens to tradition in a casino culture?

In keeping with his character, Nanapush has the last word on the land issues at Little No Horse, remarking,

> This reservation came about in a time of desperation and upon it we will see things occur more desperate yet. When I look at the scope and drift of our history, I see that we have come out of it with something, at least. This scrap of earth. This ishkonigan. This leftover. We've got this and as long as we can hold on to it we will be some sort of people.[72]

His words highlight what has been at stake all along in the fractious relationship between the Ojibwe and the U.S. government. For Nanapush, as for Lipsha, land and tradition are bound up together—just as they bind the community together. Far from being mere marks on an Indian agent's map, the reservation has come to represent Ojibwe Country, Anishinaabewakii, Indian land.

NÎPÎY / WATER

CHAPTER THREE

"An Ancient Pact, Now Broken"

Activism and Environmental Justice in
Solar Storms *and* From the River's Edge

We need new stories, new terms and conditions that are relevant to
the love of land, a new narrative . . .

—LINDA HOGAN, *Dwellings*

FOR INDIAN PEOPLE, THE MID-TWENTIETH century was one of
upheaval once again. Indian veterans returned from World War II only
to find the reservation Indian agents anxious to sign people up for a new
relocation program that would move them off the reservation into urban
centers such as Denver, San Francisco, Chicago, Dallas, and Los
Angeles. Congress terminated the tribal status of the Menominee, the
Klamath, sixty-one tribes in Oregon, and forty-one California Indian
rancherías. In 1953, Public Law 280 was enacted, transferring civil and
criminal jurisdiction over Indian land from the federal government to
the states of California, Nebraska, Minnesota, Oregon, and Wisconsin.
Another group of Indian soldiers went off to the Vietnam War, and the
American Indian Movement, founded in 1968, soon became politically
engaged in all matters concerning Native people.

As the terminated tribes worked to regain their tribal status, condemnation of Indian land under eminent domain became a new form of dispossession, despite its inherent abrogation of treaties and federal law. It
was surely with this in mind that Dakota intellectual Vine Deloria Jr. once
described federal-Indian relations in the United States as a series of land
transactions.[1]

The two novels I consider in this chapter, Linda Hogan's *Solar Storms* (1995) and Elizabeth Cook-Lynn's *From the River's Edge* (1991), are based on actual historical events involving land transactions in the mid-twentieth century between unwilling parties. These acts of Native land dispossession took the form of federal eminent domain, one in northern Canada and the other in the American West. Juxtaposing these two very different texts offers a view of two different legal systems with the same result: the illegal condemnation and appropriation of Native land. Hogan and Cook-Lynn's literary re-visions of these land narratives are powerful indictments of the effects of illegal land transfers on Native lives and lifeways. As a counterpoint to Cook-Lynn's novel, I examine contemporary responses to the consequences of the damming of the Missouri River, as depicted in Carol Burns's 2010 documentary *Mni Sose (aka Missouri River)* and in excerpts from the Oak Lake Writers' Society's 2006 volume of essays *This Stretch of the River*. Examining these texts ensures that the narrative is current, and that it covers ongoing debates over the redirection and damming of the river and the outcomes of both actions for the tribes along its route.

Critics have long recognized Hogan's fiction, poetry, and essays as important contributions to the field of ecocriticism and environmental literature. *Solar Storms* is a popular choice for classroom teaching, and it won the Colorado Book Award in 1995. In contrast, Elizabeth Cook-Lynn is widely known as a public intellectual and essayist, but her novels and poetry have failed to garner a sustained critical response. Cook-Lynn is known primarily for the political, treaty-based content of her nonfiction work, which I contend also extends to her creative work. Her work has not been recognized for having an environmental slant, yet I argue that in her fiction, as in the overarching theme of this book, Native land tenure and environmental crises are inextricably linked.

Linda Hogan's *Solar Storms* begins and ends with water. Water delivers the seventeen-year-old narrator Angel Jensen by ferry to her home village of Adam's Rib, where she looks for answers to her own story. Angel's return to the house on Poison Road marks "the end of [her] life in one America" and the beginning of another life in a fictional indigenous subsistence community, located in what appears to be the Boundary Waters region separating Minnesota from Canada.[2] This community is largely made up of women, descendants of the "abandoned ones" of the fur trade era—Cree, Anishinaabe, Fat-Eaters.[3] Here Angel reestablishes her relationship with her paternal line of grandmothers—Dora-Rouge, her great-great-grandmother; Agnes, her great-grandmother; and Bush, her step-grandmother—and with the land narratives of Adam's Rib.

There is a large body of ecocritical and environmental scholarship on *Solar Storms*, but I read it as an activist and environmental justice–oriented text. In a 1998 interview with Brad Johnson, Hogan explained her vision of the relationship between literature and activism:

> I've found that talking about issues somehow doesn't create change in the world, but if I can take one of the issues, political issues, or a tribe that's being devastated because of development—and I put it into a story, it has more of an impact. . . . People read it and they get it . . . they find characters that they can relate to and care about and they see the story from inside their own body, inside their own selves.[4]

Hogan's description of the empowering nature of literature, specifically in the form of the novel, underscores the importance of literature in and for Native communities. *Solar Storms* tells a compelling story of the human face of environmental damage and the emotional and cultural trauma caused by illegal condemnation and seizure of Native lands. Laura Virginia Castor suggests that "the narrative power of *Solar Storms* lies in its ability to create a sense of empathy[,] a politicized strategy of influencing [the] reader's attitudes and understanding of the ways in which indigenous people's rights are connected to the survival of the planet."[5] Like the proverbial miner's canary, Native and indigenous peoples' land is usually the first to be marked for large-scale projects with the potential for damage, both environmental and human. The building of dams for the generation of electric power, which both Hogan and Cook-Lynn take up in their respective novels, is one such project.

While the other texts I discuss in this book have tribally specific settings, Hogan's novel, like her other novels, is set in the territory of, and is about, a fictitious tribe. To further underscore the fictional nature of this tribal nation, Hogan includes a disclaimer at the front of the book: "This book is a work of fiction. Names, characters, places, and incidents either are products of the author's imagination or are used fictitiously. Any resemblance to actual events or locales or persons, living or dead, is entirely coincidental."[6] As Castor points out, this disclaimer protects Hogan from "potential lawsuits," and it protects the original community from seeing themselves "mirrored in her words."[7] Despite the disclaimer, critics have identified the nations and the controversy in question, especially in light of a *Missouri Review* interview Hogan gave a year before the novel was published. In the interview, Hogan explained:

> There are all kinds of restraints that you have as a writer from a particular community. You can't just assume that you know another community. Right now I'm trying to work on a book that's set in the North, but it has to be from a Chickasaw point of view because I would never pretend to presume to understand tribes up in the North, or to speak for a person of another tribe. So I'm creating a totally fictional community, and yet the story is really about the truth. It's about the history of the fur trade, and events taking place at James Bay, between the tribal governments and the Quebec government, which wants to build a dam there.[8]

Though Hogan populates her novel with the Cree and Anishinaabeg who were part of the fur trade, the Fat-Eaters, or the Beautiful People as they call themselves, are an entirely fictitious tribe. Most Native authors write about their own communities, with Hogan being a prominent exception. She undoubtedly brought attention to the James Bay situation by using the dam project as a plot device, but *Solar Storms* is not a Cree novel despite its northern setting; nor is it a Chickasaw novel, as Hogan suggests. My reason for this position is that *Solar Storms* does not take place on Chickasaw lands, but rather on fabricated ground that stands in for Cree lands. As Kelli Lyon Johnson points out, "Omitting the name of the Native nation [or inserting a fictitious one] risks accusations of what Elizabeth Cook-Lynn has called . . . 'tribelessness.'"[9] Such an approach risks the obliteration of tribal specificity, erasing the distinct cultures, languages, religions, and histories of Native nations in both the United States and Canada. *Solar Storms* makes no mention of the legal situation that allowed the seizure of land to go forward, though this is the cause of events both in the novel and in actuality. The creation of a fictitious Native community and land base is problematic for critical approaches to the text, making impossible, for example, a tribal nationalist approach. Reading the text through an activist and environmental justice lens defuses some of the critical tensions that arise with the creation of a fictitious tribe. Aligning these readings with the land narrative paradigm illuminates the human and environmental impact of the dam project, whether this impact is fictional or "truth" based.

The "truth" Hogan speaks of in her interview is subjective. It may be that she is referring to the environmental damage to the land caused by successive waves of outsiders, beginning with French fur traders in the seventeenth century and ending with the hydroelectric companies flooding Native lands in the twentieth. The ecological damage caused by flooding has included the destruction of migrating bird habitats and the deaths of thousands of migrating caribou; of smaller animals; and of numerous plants, including medicinal and food-bearing plants, brambles, and bushes. The damage to the tribal people living in this area is incalculable. As anyone researching the James Bay project will find, there are many "truths" being advocated.

Solar Storms opens in 1972, a year after Quebec prime minister Robert Bourassa announced a massive plan by Hydro-Québec, a government-owned public utility, to dam and divert all rivers running into James Bay and to build a series of reservoirs. The James Bay project provides the historical and political background for Hogan's novel.

For the Cree and Inuit bands living in the area, it meant massive flooding of their communities and hunting lands—and relocation. The project site lies 660 miles north of Montreal, between the forty-ninth and fifty-fifth parallels. These lands are unceded territory, and they have not been the subject of any treaty. Yet Canadian law explicitly states that "all major projects built north of the 49th parallel are exempt from public hearings, requiring only the provincial environment minister's approval."[10] The Cree and Inuit communities first noticed the Hydro-Québec project when the access road to James Bay was built. In June 1971, a meeting was held at the Cree community of Mistassini; it was the first entry into Canada's political process that the Cree had ever known. The result of this initial meeting was a petition to the minister of Indian Affairs, declaring in part:

> We, the representatives of the Cree bands that will be affected by the James Bay hydro project or any other project, oppose to these projects because we believe that only the beavers have the right to build dams in our territory.[11]

The Cree bands' petition is an example of the ongoing pact between humans and their other-than-human relatives, one that was still intact in 1971. The pact is part of the nehiyaw weyeswewna, or the Cree laws governing their relationship with the world around them. The building of the James Bay hydro project marked the beginning of environmental damage in the north, and the beginning of a broken pact.

André Picard writes that when the Caniapiscau River was diverted to create the LG4 reservoir, "the earth's crust shifted, causing a mild tremor," even though that reservoir was one of the smallest in the plan.[12] The Caniapiscau, like many northern rivers, flowed south to north until the James Bay project began; it "is one of nineteen ancient waterways that has been or will be altered in an unprecedented geographic manipulation."[13] Even more worrisome is the mercury that was released from the bedrock during flooding, which made its way up the food chain into the Cree diet. Methyl mercury poisoning, or nimass aksiwin, in fish has devastated the traditional food staple of the Cree and their subsistence way of life. Most people in Chisasibi, a new community built when the smaller villages were flooded, have unacceptably high levels of mercury in their systems.[14]

The James Bay projects garnered little attention from the United States, and even from southern Canada. Jan Beyea of the National Audubon Society notes, "In terms of wildlife and habitat, the devastation of James Bay is the northern equivalent of the destruction of the tropical rainforest."[15] There are now new projects north of the forty-ninth parallel that are equally destructive, such as the tar sands of Alberta and the Keystone XL pipeline.

Adam's Rib, as Angel describes, "was in the north country, the place where water was broken apart by land, land split open by water so that the maps showed places both bound and, if you knew the way in, boundless. The elders said it was where land and water had joined together in an ancient pact, now broken."[16] There is an inherent violence in Angel's description, a breaking, a splitting, a binding that has an echo in the name of the village, resonant with the biblical story of Eve's creation.[17] Violence has also left its mark on Angel. She wears her hair "down over the right side of her face" to cover the "scars that had shaped [her] life."[18] In another broken pact, Angel's scars were caused by her mother, Hannah Wing. They are the reason for Angel's removal from Adam's Rib so many years before.

The Boundary Waters region of which Adam's Rib is a part represents many things at once. It forms a political space, dubbed "the Triangle," which the United States, Canada, and several tribal nations seek control over. It is a permeable boundary between landmasses and nation-states, although it is only navigable for those who can read its ever-shifting narrative. Within the context of the novel, Adam's Rib is the center of the world, situated in the midst of the broken pact. It is here where Angel "learn[s] water," where she learns to swim, paddle, and steer, to cross boundaries between water and land, and between worlds.[19]

The broken pact between land and water is just one of a number of such broken pacts. John Husk tells Angel, "There had once been a covenant between animals and men. . . . They would care for one another. It was an agreement much like the one between land and water. This pact, too, had been broken, forced by need and hunger."[20] These pacts, which are based on traditional indigenous knowledge, form part of the land narratives of Adam's Rib and the surrounding land and waterways. Poisson Road may have received its original name when small fish rained down from the sky, but mispronunciation and environmental damage have resulted in a name change in concert with the change in the land narrative—it is now called Poison Road. These narratives form the key to Angel's personal narrative and her link to her mother. Her great-grandmother, Agnes Iron, tells Angel, "Nobody knows where it began, your story. . . . What happened to you started long ago. It began around the time of the killing of the wolves. When people were starving. . . . There wasn't a single beaver that year. And they'd just logged the last of the pine forests."[21] It is noteworthy that Agnes begins Angel's story with the words "Nobody knows where it began." As is the case in Keith Basso's Cibecue Apache narratives, *where* something happens is the most significant part of the story. Angel's story does not begin with her birth, but with a series of environmental crises that occurred long before, caused by colonization: the clear-cutting of forests; the overhunting caused by the fur trade; and the killing of wolves, the natural predators of the settlers' cattle. Angel's personal narrative merges with the land's narrative and its environmental crises. These crises, Hogan seemingly asserts, are caused by "broken pacts" with water, land, and animals.

There are other broken pacts that similarly cause crises of a more personal nature: Loretta Wing's abuse by unknown men and her later coercion into prostitution; Harold's desertion of his wife, Bush; Loretta's abuse of her daughter, Hannah; and Hannah's abuse of her own daughter, Angel. Loretta appears in Adam's Rib by boat, smelling of almonds, an olfactory clue to the residue of cyanide, which places her as one of the "Elk Islanders, who ate the poisoned carcasses of deer that the settlers left out for the wolves."[22] Hannah also emerges from the water at

Adam's Rib, empty-eyed and with a faint smell of almonds, suggesting that she, too, has been a victim of abuse. These personal crises are entwined with the environmental and legal crises, suggesting that the manner in which humans treat each other and their other-than-human relatives has consequences for the land itself. The events outlined by Agnes are related to resource extraction, which leaves the land barren and poisoned.

Yet before these crises occurred, the world was created, and it is the world that forms the foundation of the land narrative. Tulik, an elder from the Fat-Eaters, tells Angel their creation story, which starts with water covering the world.[23] The only being was Beaver, who "took trees down from the sky, brought up pebbles and clay from the waters, broke the ice," and made land.[24] Beaver created humans, and then made a pact with them. In exchange for fish, waterfowl, and animals, humans would take care of the world. This was the original pact; it was ultimately broken, leaving openings for other broken pacts. The beaver takes on an important role in *Solar Storms*, especially in Bush's study of ancient maps. She says of Western mapmakers, "None of them ever considered how beavers change the land."[25] R. M. Baxter notes that beaver dams "can cause spectacular changes in certain areas."[26] Beaver brought land and humans into being, and continues to leave his/her signature on the land's narrative.

The action of the novel shifts from Angel's adjustment to this new land to the arrival of two young men in a canoe, who bring disconcerting news—the government plans to build dams and reservoirs in the Fat-Eaters' territory. After Bush passes the winter studying ancient maps of the north, she, Angel, Agnes, and Dora-Rouge embark on a canoe journey through the Boundary Waters into Canada. They are women with a mission: Dora-Rouge is going to her ancestral territory to die; Agnes is accompanying her mother, Dora-Rouge; Angel is seeking her own mother, who, she has heard, is in the north; and Bush is going to protest the construction of the dams. Their journey is marked by a changing landscape. Rivers have been diverted by the hydroelectric plan, leaving mud flats in their wake; other rivers are churning with force.

In one important scene, they encounter the Se Nay River, which has already been channelized. High stone walls hold the river's force. Because the river is impossible to pass on foot, the women nearly turn back. Dora-Rouge convinces them to let her speak to the river, to ask its permission to let them pass through safely. She tosses tobacco into the roiling waters as an offering. Dora-Rouge's negotiation with the river has unintended consequences, as Agnes dies not long after they make their way down the river. Hogan does not allow either the reader or the other characters to be privy to Dora-Rouge's words, despite the ancientness of the practice of Native and indigenous peoples asking permission of, and offering tobacco to, bodies of waters before embarking on a journey. In the fictional world Hogan has created, "there was a place inside the human that spoke with land. . . . They dreamed charts of land and currents of water."[27] As Agnes comments ironically, "It used to be that you could even strike a bargain with the weather."[28] Agnes uses the past tense, suggesting that such bargains are no longer possible, because of either changes in the weather or the void left by those who possessed such knowledge. T. Christine Jespersen contends that "Hogan reconfigures adventure as a mode of activism based upon indigenous belief about resistance and the essential connections between humans and nature."[29] Hogan reworks the Western-male adventure narrative of canoeing into wild unknown spaces, especially as these are four generations of women making the trip.[30] The "wild unknown spaces" are only so because of the dam construction and the diversion of the rivers. Dora-Rouge knows these waterways, but they have been manipulated and reversed until they are now almost illegible.

In Two-Town, the women's final destination, the landscape has already been changed by logging machines and backhoes. Bush's old navigation maps are replaced by the hydroelectric company's new maps, which show the diverting of rivers and the creation of reservoirs. As Angel narrates, "It was a raw and scarred place, a land that had learned to survive, even to thrive, on harshness. . . . The animals were no longer there, nor were the people or clans, the landmarks, not even the enormous sturgeon . . . not the water they once swam in. Most of the trees had become nothing more than large mounds of sawdust."[31] During Dora-Rouge's admittedly long lifetime, the land of the Fat-Eaters has been transformed from a forested, resource-filled environment to one in which all resources have been extracted, thus changing its narrative. A subsistence style of living is no longer possible in the region. Most of the people who remain in Two-Town are "people in pain . . . with puffy faces and empty eyes. It was murder of the soul that was taking place here."[32] Dora-Rouge's question is an important one: "[H]ow do conquered people get back their lives? She and others knew the protest against the dams and river diversions was their only hope. Those who protested were the ones who could still believe they might survive as a people."[33] This last phrase underscores the unifying nature of land for a nation's culture, history, and people. Protecting the land against the dams and its diversions means protecting the land narratives, "the storied land" that makes a people distinct from others—that makes them who they are.[34]

It is here in Two-Town that Angel finally meets her birth mother, Hannah Wing. What she sees in Hannah is "more ruined than the land."[35] Hannah denies ever hitting Angel, which may be true, but the evidence on Angel's face—tooth marks, burns, marks from hot wires— reveals violence. Hannah's home to the north is even more desperate than Two-Town. The land is pocked by bombing ranges used by military planes, and by half-built roads and burnt-out areas; there is no evidence of animal life. The damaged landscape mirrors Hannah's emotional and psychological damage. Hannah's slow death fills Angel with "grief and compassion," which frees Angel from her own scars, both internal and external.[36] Angel has been healed through her interactions with the land and waterways of the Boundary Waters, through the canoe journey, and through her relationship with her grandmothers. Her having been healed prepares Angel to take charge of Hannah's infant daughter, whom Angel names Aurora, and thus enables her to stop violence from being passed down to the next generation. Aurora, of course, means dawn, connoting new beginnings. It may also be a reference to the aurora borealis, or northern lights, which are sacred to many northern tribes.

The government sends in the military to shut down the protests at Two-Town. This takes place in 1973, the year of the siege at Wounded Knee in South Dakota, a historical event Hogan draws from in her depiction of the Two-Town protests. At the height of the siege at Two-Town, Angel leaves with a feverish Aurora; as the youngest of the protesters, they are considered the future, and therefore they must be protected. Their return to Adam's Rib reveals a changed landscape. Flooding downstream has already occurred as a result of the northern hydro plan. Angel adds to the land narrative, declaring, "It was against the will of land, I knew, to turn rivers into lakes, lakes into dry land, to send rivers along new paths. I hoped the earth would one day forgive this breach of faith, the broken agreements humans had with it."[37]

Tulik's creation story and Angel's arrival at Adam's Rib both begin with water; Angel's return to Adam's Rib is also a return to water. Though floods and the recession of floodwaters are natural events, the story Hogan retells in *Solar Storms* is not a story of nature, but of man's manipulation of nature, which changes the pact between the people and the land. The flow of rivers in northern Canada has as much to do with the "flow of power in history" as it does in the American West.[38]

Whereas Hogan's *Solar Storms* is based on an actual event but told through a fictional tribe, Elizabeth Cook-Lynn's 1991 novel *From the River's Edge* is set firmly within a Dakotah context on the Crow Creek Sioux Reservation in South Dakota. The novel centers on rancher John Tatekeya's attempt to seek restitution through federal court for forty-two head of stolen cattle. The litigation results in the conviction of the son of Tatekeya's white neighbor, but the cattle are long gone (and a criminal case such as this rarely results in restitution). During the trial, through the testimony of witnesses, Tatekeya loses his honor and good name in front of family, friends, and community members. An extramarital affair between Tatekeya and a younger woman, Aurelia Blue, is uncovered in the testimony. Even more alarming are the actions of

Jason Big Pipe, the son of Tatekaya's ceremonial relative, who defies kinship rules to testify for the defendant. Jason's testimony is intended to cover up the involvement of his brother, Sheridan, in the theft of the cattle. The trial causes a rupture in Tatekeya's relationship with Jason's father, Harvey Big Pipe, who stops attending ceremonies to avoid him.

Tatekeya's lawyer explains to him that the court case "is not about the stolen cattle, but about justice and the law . . . in terms of what is *fair*."[39] This discrepancy between Western notions of "justice" and what is "fair" on the one hand, and Dakotah beliefs and values on the other, is at the heart of Cook-Lynn's novel. In fact, the lawyer's words mirror the historical events that provide the context for the novel: the damming of the Missouri River and the flooding of twenty-three reservations under the Pick-Sloan Plan. These also weigh the discrepancies between "justice" and what is "fair."

Under the Pick-Sloan Plan, the U.S. Army Corps of Engineers, part of whose mission was at one time to "defend America against floods,"[40] "built five main-stem projects that destroyed over 550 square miles of tribal land in North and South Dakota and dislocated more than nine hundred Indian families."[41] Army dams on the Missouri flooded more than 202,000 acres of Sioux tribal lands. The Crow Creek Reservation was flooded twice, first by the Fort Randall Dam, completed in 1956, and then by the Big Bend Dam, completed in 1966. The hardest hit of all of the South Dakota reservations, the Crow Creek Reservation lost over fifteen thousand acres of land. Over one hundred families, representing almost 40 percent of the population, were forced to relocate to less desirable home sites. Along with the acreage, "loss of primary fuel, food, and water resources, and primary grazing land effectively destroyed the Indians' economic base."[42] As with the Cree of James Bay, the Sioux were unaware of the Pick-Sloan Plan until it had already been approved. According to Michael Lawson,

> The Bureau of Indian Affairs was fully informed, yet made no objections to the plan while it was being debated in Congress in 1944. . . . The Corps of Engineers was so confident that it could

acquire the Indian land it needed through federal powers of eminent domain that it began construction on its dams, including
those actually on reservation property, even before opening formal
negotiations with the tribal leaders. The legislation establishing the
Pick-Sloan Plan also ignored the Indians' water rights under the
so-called Winters Doctrine.[43]

The Winters Doctrine stemmed from a 1908 U.S. Supreme Court case,
Winters v. United States, which pertained to upstream farmers' diverting
of the Milk River into dams and reservoirs for irrigation use, leaving
insufficient water for the downstream Gros Ventre and Assiniboine
tribes of Montana's Fort Belknap Reservation. The Department of the
Interior, which comprises the Bureau of Indian Affairs, brought an
injunction against Winters and the other defendants on behalf of the
Fort Belknap tribes. The defendants appealed. Each higher court found
that the tribes' entitlement to water was reserved by treaty rights; in this
case those rights were set forth during the 1888 founding of the Fort
Belknap Reservation. The Supreme Court further held that federal law
trumps state law, preventing state doctrines of prior appropriation from
extinguishing Native water rights.[44]

In total, the U.S. Army Corps took over 1.6 million acres of Indian
land as part of the Pick-Sloan Plan, forcing more than 25 percent of the
four thousand families involved to go to court for restitution.[45] Those
families that did enter into litigation with the Corps were met with hos-
tility and intimidation, as does John Tatekeya during his experience
with the federal court. Ultimately, any benefits of flood control were
outweighed by the price paid by the Native people involved in order to
make the project possible.[46] While one of the main purposes of the Pick-
Sloan Plan was to generate electricity, many Sioux villages still remain,
for the most part, without it.

Part of the condemnation process under eminent domain is consideration of the public good. The concept of the public good infers what is
"just" and "fair." The dams and reservoirs were meant to control the
flooding of downstream cities, create electricity, and provide recreational

opportunities such as boating and fishing. The inhabitants of the twenty-three reservations impacted by these dams do not all have electricity, and few, if any, are in a financial position to enjoy boating and other such activities.

From the River's Edge begins with a preface in which the author, Elizabeth Cook-Lynn, relates,

> I stood on a hill with Big Pipe and watched the flooding waters of the Missouri River Power Project unleash the river's power. . . . As old Pipe grieved, the water covered the trees of a timber stand which had nourished a people for all generations, and it took twenty years for those trees to die, their skeletons still and white. It took much less time for the snakes and small animals to disappear. Today, old Pipe has a hard time finding the root which cures his toothache, and he tells everyone that it is the white man's determination to change the river which accounts for the destruction of all life's forms.[47]

The author's witnessing of the flooding of the Crow Creek Dakota lands functions as a testament to the government's failure to adhere to the Supreme Court's ruling in *Winters v. United States*.[48] In other words, under eminent domain law the condemnation of these lands is illegal, as they are protected by treaty rights. This relatively short passage contains images evoking the environmental and spiritual devastation on the Crow Creek Reservation, damage that is likely not quantifiable in the eyes of the Corps or the courts. The river is home to the unktechi water spirits, making its loss as spiritual as it is environmental and material.[49]

The flooding of the land challenges the very essence of the Dakotah nation. Cook-Lynn writes, "The indigenous view of the world [holds]—that the very origins of a people are specifically tribal (nationalistic) and rooted in a specific geography (place), that mythology (soul) and geography (land) are inseparable, that even language is rooted in a specific place."[50] In Cook-Lynn's indigenous view of the world, if geography or land is at risk, then so are mythology and language. As Tatekeya asks himself, "Who would his children be? Where would they live?"[51]

Tatekeya is a witness to this cataclysmic event in Dakotah tribal history, having seen "his mother's allotment . . . and many, many more disappear under the great body of water; thousands of acres of homelands all up and down the river which had nourished the people, now gone. . . . And the world was again changed forever."[52] The flooding of the homelands takes its place in tribal history next to the Treaty of Fort Laramie, the loss of the Black Hills, the establishment of the reservation system, and the Allotment Act as world-shifting events. The diversion of the Missouri's flow changes the characters' world in small and large ways. For example, Tatekeya's wife, Rose, asks him, "'What is happening, John?' as she returns from hunting the ti(n)psina." She presses, "It has moved and now I can find it nowhere. Do you think that it has disappeared for good?'" and the narrator elaborates that "[i]t was a time when his wife nearly gave up, a time of great stress, waste, and confusion."[53] Just as the river has changed its narrative, so too have the edible roots and medicinal plants changed their narratives in the wake of events that were once unthinkable.

The trial demonstrates that it is not only the land, river, and animal and plant life that have shifted courses. The people have as well. The narrator relates Tatekeya's recollection of Jason Big Pipe's testimony:

> [H]e knew that for some the old, familial bonds of respect for one another, those significant communal codes of behavior as old as the tribes themselves, were no longer held as intrinsically valuable. It began long ago, he now believed. But because of the recent flooding of the homelands, the constant moving about and resettlement, and the repeated destruction of the places where the people were born and buried for century upon century, one generation upon the next generation, it was now a crucial matter.[54]

The loss of the Dakotah homelands is almost too much to bear, threatening as it does the very underpinnings of their ways. The "communal codes of behavior" are what make Tatekeya and his people Dakotah. Cook-Lynn stated in an interview that "the most terrible crime that can be committed in Sioux culture, in Dakotah culture, is to commit a crime against one's own relatives and against one's own brother."[55] Jason Big Pipe has not only committed a crime within the context of Dakotah culture, but he has also perjured himself and slandered Tatekeya in federal court. Too, he is guilty of aiding and abetting a crime of property. For Jason, the tension lies in conflicting loyalties.

After the trial, the hay stored in Tatekeya's outbuildings is set on fire, threatening to burn down his home. Once the fire has been extinguished with the help of neighbors, Tatekeya asks one of the men for his opinion on what "started all this," and the narrator expounds,

> He [Tatekeya] was speaking philosophically about the flooding of his lands, the disappearance of life forms along the river, the trial and subsequent fire, the historical thefts of land from his people, and the agony of existence without the support of Benno. In his thoughts were the words of Gray Plume and all of the grandfathers who had said that life in accordance with the white man's ways was indecent.[56]

This paragraph, perhaps the most central in the novel, brings together land theft, the disregard for treaty rights, and environmental devastation. The passage is linked to a previous meditation by Tatekeya on the tenuous survival of Dakotah communal codes of behavior, and "the idea that what distinguished the Dakotapi from all others in this world was the powerful and compelling individual sense of obligation toward one's relatives."[57] Together, these passages suggest that without the homelands, the communal codes of behavior are already starting to disappear. Tatekeya's own elders—among them his grandfather Gray Plume and his mentor Benno—have walked on, and he must now rely on their teachings as a guide.

Jason Big Pipe, who has helped put out the blaze, tells Tatekeya that the fire was started by the same white neighbor who stole his cattle. Jason admits that his brother, Sheridan, helped the neighbor load up the cattle and threatened Jason with violence if he did not lie for them. His moral dilemma, then, centered on whether he should commit a crime against a ceremonial relative or his own brother. Jason's admission to Tatekeya is an attempt to make things right, to restore "justice" and explain what is "fair." He sums up his admission by asking, "And, hell, I couldn't let my brother go to the pen, could I?"[58] Tatekeya has no answer to this question, which shakes him to his very core. The Western concepts of "justice" and what is "fair" are at odds with Dakotah belief systems, in an echo of Gray Plume's warning "that an unjust world would make it impossible for his grandchildren to live just lives."[59] In the aftermath of the trial and the fire, Tatekeya turns to Rose, saying, "'We are the children of Gray Plume,'" the narrator elaborating, "He said it in confidence. Not in defeat or sorrow, but matter-of-factly."[60] As the children of Gray Plume, they will endure within the Dakotah way of life.

The novel's brief epilogue depicts Tatekeya and Harvey Big Pipe in a sweat lodge ceremony, which requires that any disagreement between the two be put aside. Big Pipe's young grandson also takes part, a sign that perhaps younger generations will continue these ceremonial practices on the new land.

The multiple losses—cultural, spiritual, linguistic, and epistemological—sustained in the decades since the completion of the Hydro-Québec and Pick-Sloan projects have not abated. Names of plants and their uses not only fade from memory once growing spaces have been flooded out, but they disappear from everyday language as well. Environmental and health issues are closely linked, as Michael Lawson points out in Carol Burns's 2010 documentary *Mni Sose (aka Missouri River)*: "[I]n the bottomlands you had all the resources you needed for subsistence. The tribes were moved further out onto the prairie where vital things had to be bought or didn't exist anymore."[61] Lawson's comment is echoed by tribal members participating in the documentary, who live along the Missouri River. Cheyenne River Sioux elder and registered nurse

Marcella Lebeau links the increase in rates of obesity, alcoholism, diabetes, and suicide to the devastation caused by having to leave the homelands for alien territory at Eagle Butte, South Dakota. Most poignantly, Three Affiliated Tribes member Pemina Yellow Bird states, "I'm a member of the first generation to grow up not knowing what our homelands looked like."[62]

As Lydia Whirlwind Soldier (Rosebud Sioux) points out in the dialogue among the Oak Lake Writers' Society, "Disrupting the river disrupted a way of life and a way of transferring knowledge. It broke a link."[63] Also disrupted are the stories, the land narratives. Gladys Hawk (Standing Rock Sioux) explains:

> The change in environment has also affected our stories—stories associated with the river. But now, with the way the water is, say, and twenty years down the line, are there going to be stories on that same level—of, say Inktomi—that were associated with all of these elements of the surrounding area, the land and everything? They won't be the same and so it has affected that possibility. Let me give you an example. Inktomi stories about coyote, rabbit, and others— common stories that were native to us—were associated with all of the natural elements. They came out of the natural environment that we were familiar with. But if you take away the natural world as we knew it, you can no longer create or tell those stories. You can't tell the stories anymore to younger generations because those animals are no longer there to be used to tell the stories in order to teach the values those stories were intended to teach.[64]

Hawk neatly sums up the relationship between specific landscapes and their narratives, which affects not only the tribes along the Missouri River but also the Cree and Inuit living in the James Bay region. The massive projects that changed the courses of rivers and flooded acres upon acres of land have long been completed, but the devastation they have wrought, in both human and environmental terms, continues to this day.

CHAPTER FOUR

Climate Change as Indigenous Dispossession for the Twenty-First Century

The United Houma Nation of Louisiana and the Alaska Native Villages of Kivalina and Shishmaref

There is a word circulating amidst politicians and scientists now that Native people have heard before: *relocation*.

—THOMAS MAYHEART DARDAR JR.,
Principal Chief, United Houma Nation

People from the outside don't understand. They don't know our story.

—LORA ANN CHAISSON, United Houma Nation

AS THE EPIGRAPH FROM UNITED Houma Nation Principal Chief Thomas Mayheart Dardar Jr. suggests, relocation in the twenty-first century is not the forced removal at bayonet point by U.S. armed forces of the early nineteenth century, yet it looms nightmarishly ahead for the United Houma Nation in Louisiana and the Alaska Native villages of Kivalina and Shishmaref. Despite their differences in location, language, culture, history, population size, and status of recognition by the federal government, the United Houma Nation, Kivalina, and Shishmaref are facing similar situations in general terms of the coastal erosion and storm intensification brought about in part by climate

89

change. One more major hurricane making landfall, one more major Arctic storm, and these Native communities run the risk of seeing their land literally wash away, their people evacuate and disperse, and their cultures fragment.

In such dire times, who stops to write a poem, a piece of short fiction, or a novel? The stories, of course, do not stop; instead, they gain a particular urgency not necessarily suited to belletristic literature. Older stories about animals and sea ice have attained greater relevance now that the coastal ice formations that once protected the Alaska Native villages from Arctic storm surges are forming later and melting earlier. Many families have stories of surviving past hurricanes; their future stories are now foreshadowed by the latest developments in the theoretical modeling of tropical storms and hurricanes. New narratives in the form of scientific reports and computerized tracking now mingle with older land narratives. And Native communities have turned to new forms of media to tell their survival stories to a worldwide audience.

For the United Houma Nation (UHN), a state-recognized tribe in southeastern coastal Louisiana, the landfall of Hurricane Katrina on August 29, 2005, could be said to have marked the beginning of a wide-reaching crisis. Ninety percent of the tribe's seventeen thousand members live within a six-parish (Terrebonne, Lafourche, Jefferson, St. Mary, St. Bernard, and Plaquemines) service area encompassing 4,570 square miles.[1] Within this area, long-standing tribal communities such as Pointe-aux-Chenes, Isle de Jean Charles, Dulac, and Golden Meadow are situated among the interwoven bayous where the Houma people traditionally earned their living by fishing, trapping, and hunting. Although by land and road these communities are distant, they were historically very close by water.[2] The majority of the communities lie at or below sea level, placing them at risk for storm surges and flooding. Today, the United Houma Nation faces some of the most significant environmental problems in North America, including coastal erosion, rising sea levels, salt water intrusion, and the intensification of storm dynamics; when coupled with the effects of the 2010 BP Deep-water Horizon blowout, these create a "perfect storm" that threatens the very ground the Houma live on and the very waterways where they make their living. In many ways, this is one of the biggest environmental stories that no one has heard of. It begins with the Mississippi River, thousands of years ago.

The headwaters of the Mississippi are found at Lake Itasca in northern Minnesota, not far from the White Earth Reservation. The trickle of the river is small enough to step over, which is the touristy thing to do when visiting Itasca State Park. There is no hint of the muddy and mighty river that will pick up speed and width as it flows southward some 2,552 miles toward the Mississippi Delta, where it offers up sediment-rich alluvial deposits before emptying into the Gulf of Mexico. What we now know of as coastal Louisiana is new land, made from sediment continuously laid down by the great Mississippi over the course of thousands of years. Like the Anishinaabe creation story retold in the introduction to this book, the Mississippi River Delta is, according to Ivor Van Heerden, a "dynamic interplay of land and water," with "new lands . . . continuously built and old lands changed and lost."[3] These new lands make up four million acres of marshes, swamps, and estuaries in Louisiana, totaling 40 percent of all of the coastal wetlands in the forty-eight contiguous states. Louisiana's coastal wetlands are home to diverse wildlife and plant life, migratory birds, and natural fisheries, making them one of the world's most diverse and complex ecosystems.[4]

It is here in the marshes, swamps, and bayous of southeastern coastal Louisiana that members of the United Houma Nation have made their home since 1709, when they were forced out of their ancestral village near present-day Angola by hostile tribes. They settled in Bayou LaFourche.[5] This forced relocation was the Houma Nation's first experience of adapting to a new environment—although it would not be their last—and of leaving behind their major agricultural practices and ceremonies for new practices and ceremonies revolving around water. Their lives and land have been shaped by water, and yet water may prove their undoing. The United Houma Nation is now fighting to survive as a people and a distinct cultural and political entity.

While Louisiana's wetlands are the "fastest disappearing landmass on earth," this distinction did not materialize overnight.[6] The wetlands' disappearance is the result of a complex combination of climatic, economic, and historical events, beginning with the 1722 construction of the first artificial levees along the Mississippi River, built in New Orleans to stop natural springtime flooding. Reliance on levee systems grew exponentially as New Orleans became an important international port and economic engine in the Gulf region. By the early 1900s, not only had city officials constructed more miles of levees along the river, but they had also begun to drain and fill the wetlands between New Orleans and Lake Pontchartrain for development. This drain-and-fill approach was typical at the time, when swamps, marshes, and other types of wetlands were viewed as the sources of vapors and "bad air" that gave rise to illness and disease.[7] It also caused soil subsidence, or the sinking of the swamp's peat soil. Levee construction took on a force of its own after New Orleans's Great Flood of 1927, memorialized by the blues song "When the Levee Breaks," by Kansas Joe McCoy and Memphis Minnie.[8] The U.S. Army Corps of Engineers was charged with protecting New Orleans with a new system of levees and navigation controls under the Flood Control Act of 1928. As more levees were built, less sediment was deposited into the wetlands, hastening the coastline's natural erosion and the soil's subsidence.[9] The flood protection systems, together with the machinery of the oil and gas industry, were negatively impacting Louisiana's wetlands regions long before Hurricane Katrina made herself known.

In 1901, oil and gas drilling began in Louisiana, with much of it taking place in the isolated bayous of the southeastern portion of the state. Between 1901 and 1980, the industry laid some eighty thousand miles of pipelines and dredged ninety-three thousand miles of navigation canals over an expanse of wetlands that once covered 3.2 million acres.[10] These navigation canals put into effect a chain of events that is in full force today: The canals allow salt water intrusion from the Gulf of

Mexico into the freshwater marshes. The salt water begins killing off trees and aquatic marsh grasses. As plants die, their roots are no longer able to serve as a buffer against soil erosion, literally causing the land to disappear. Loss of plant life leads to loss of spawning grounds for fish, shrimp, and crabs.

Many of these canals have been abandoned as the wells have gone dry. With no new sediment to fill them in, navigation canals double their width every fourteen years. Factor in subsidence and the deterioration of marshlands caused by grasses dying from the "brown marsh" phenomenon (the unseasonal and rapid browning of intertidal smooth cordgrass marshes, which began in the spring of 2000), and the end result is more open water than marshland.[11] In addition to being an ecological and environmental disaster, this threatens Louisiana's multibillion-dollar fishing industry.

The marshes, swamps, and other wetlands serve another purpose— they protect against storm surges. Every three- to four-mile region of healthy marshland reduces storm surges by one foot.[12] In other words, healthy, robust wetlands weaken storms as they move inland, serving as buffers for coastal communities. The current condition of its wetlands not only exposes Louisiana to coastal erosion caused by hurricanes, but it also places the state in greater danger from global climate change than any other place in the United States. Dr. Robert Twilley, the director of the Center for Ecology and Environmental Technology at the University of Louisiana at Lafayette, explains, "Because of the sedimentary composition of our deltaic plain, deeper regions of our marshes are sinking at the same time that the sea level is rising. So Louisiana can expect a combined, or relative, sea-level rise of at least fifteen inches in the next one hundred years—and up to forty-four inches in some places."[13] In other words, because sediment deposited by the river into marshes compacts over time, and because the sea level is rising as a result of glacial melt and other factors at the same time, the Louisiana coastline will eventually be underwater.

As Principal Chief Thomas Mayheart Dardar Jr. made clear in his testimony before the U.S. Senate Committee on Indian Affairs in July 2012,

Each year, twenty-five square miles of wetlands—or a football field every half hour—is lost. . . . Places where our tribal members used to walk to visit a neighbor, they now have to boat. Roads once built up on land are now covered in water. Electricity poles that were once along that road are now in water. It is our tribal members that live along those swamps, fish these waters, hunt this marshland and depend on the land that is disappearing.[14]

At this current rate, by the year 2040, Louisiana will have lost more than one million acres of coastal wetlands since 1978.[15]

For Michael T. Mayheart Dardar, hurricanes were a part of life while growing up in Houma Nation territory in Golden Meadow, Louisiana. There were smaller storms, of course, but there were also large, forceful storms such as Hurricane Betsy, which wiped out Dardar's family home in 1965, when he was a small boy. The Dardars rebuilt their home and their lives, only to see their home wiped out again in 1969 by Hurricane Camille. Once again, the family rebuilt. Dardar remembers his early years as a time when Houma men were primarily hunters, trappers, and commercial fishermen. More important, it was a time when the marshlands and swamps were healthier and the coastlines more secure. It was a time when people were able to rebuild their lives.[16]

The Houma people's relationship with hurricanes and floods can be traced through their raised, or "stilt," houses, which have been raised progressively higher as the years have gone by. Leah Savoy, a United Houma Nation tribal member living on Isle de Jean Charles in Terrebonne Parish, points out that as of 2010, the combination of rising sea levels and coastal erosion means "[you] cannot put a home there unless you are seventeen feet in the air."[17] Isle de Jean Charles was once a place where pecan, fig, and persimmon trees grew, but now, Savoy notes, the trees are black stumps rising out of the water.

The turning point for the Houma people came with Hurricane Katrina on August 29, 2005, followed by Hurricane Rita a mere three weeks later. Houma lands lay at the intersection of the two storms, which flooded the homes of 80 percent of tribal members. By 2005, more coastline had disappeared; marshlands were disappearing. Houma communities were now at the edge of the gulf. As former principal chief Brenda Dardar Robichaux explained in an interview, "Our tribal communities along the bayous used to look out the back doors of their homes and see land, but now they see only water. When the hurricanes come in to the Gulf, there are no natural barriers to slow them down and protect our communities."[18] From the effects of Katrina and Rita alone, 217 more square miles of land were lost, devastated by storm surges and coastal erosion.

While the nation's eyes were riveted by New Orleans and its Superdome, the people of the United Houma Nation were digging out of the debris, mud, and muck left behind when the floodwaters retreated. The Houma Nation formed emergency crews to account for their members and begin the cleanup process. They received little to no press coverage—and, because of their status as a tribe without federal recognition, little to no assistance from government agencies. (The tribe was recognized by the state of Louisiana in 1979.) Many older Houma tribal members do not speak fluent English, and they were unable to fill out the complicated FEMA forms for additional help. Too, as David Holthouse and Priscilla Holthouse note, "Jim Crow laws prevented Houma children from attending public schools until the mid-1960s, and the few [existing] 'Indian schools' only went up to the seventh grade," which resulted in educational and language barriers for certain demographics of the tribe.[19] The Native media stepped up to publicize the situation, and other media outlets in turn picked up the story. The National Congress of American Indians chartered a helicopter on behalf of the Houma, flying Robichaux and several tribal council members over the devastated Plaquemines Parish to assess the damage. "We became physically ill when we saw our community in this Parish," Robichaux remembers. "The village of thirty families had nothing left—peoples' homes looked like they never existed; their homes were simply gone."[20] Robichaux began the United Houma Nation Relief Fund with donations from other Native nations, from churches, and from people across the

United States. Work began on rebuilding, especially for the elders of the tribe. Still, as Robichaux points out, "Life as we knew it changed."[21]

Hurricanes Gustav and Ike in 2008 and Hurricane Isaac in 2012 were additional harsh blows to the Houma communities, not only causing more land erosion, but also wiping out tribal members' livelihoods. Commercial fishermen, trappers, and subsistence hunters require land; so do the people who live in these coastal areas. While scientists debate the relationship between climate change and hurricanes, it is apparent that what we are seeing is an intensification of storm dynamics. As the amount of open water grows, winds build larger waves, which strike shorelines with greater force, increasing the rate of erosion. And that results in exponential acceleration—the larger the problem gets, the faster it gets even larger. Many have lost a great deal of land to these cycles of erosion, subsidence, and rising sea levels.

During Hurricane Isaac in 2012, the tribal headquarters building lost its roof, hampering recovery efforts. The tribe relied on social media networks such as Facebook to make contact with tribal members and to disseminate relief information. Rather than rebuild, some families have relocated.

The narrative of the United Houma Nation and its loss of land and viable wetlands circles back to oil—the oil industry's abandoned navigation canals continue to disrupt the Houma environment. On April 20, 2010, the BP-owned Deepwater Horizon drilling rig exploded, sending an estimated fifty-three thousand barrels of oil per day gushing out into the Gulf of Mexico. The rig was finally capped three months later. The most immediate consequence for the Houma Nation was the premature end of fishing season, which many tribal members depend on for a living. Many Houma fishermen lost jobs, incomes, and subsistence practices because of the spill. The oil and chemical dispersants eventually reached the marshes and wetlands, causing plant life to die out—thereby further hastening erosion. Many shrimping grounds have also died out, and those that haven't are seeing other types of problems. Dean Blanchard, a seafood wholesaler from Grand Isle, reported:

We're seeing all kinds of problems, shrimp with no eyes and no baby fish. Boats are reporting five and six dead dolphins a day. Our beach is producing less than 1 percent of the shrimp (of normal catches). Grand Isle used to be the best fishing grounds in the country. Our bay is full of oil and our beach is dead[;] they've used so many dispersants. . . . I don't think we'll have a fishing industry here in two or three years. Everyone is running out of money. . . . I'd rather have 100 Katrinas than one BP spill.[22]

Perhaps even more frightening are the effects of the chemical dispersants on humans. According to Gina M. Solomon and Sarah Janssen, the oil spill and dispersants "pose direct threats from inhalation and dermal contact."[23] In the first days of the cleanup process, three hundred people, most of them cleanup workers, sought medical care for symptoms ranging from dizziness to nausea, headaches, vomiting, and respiratory distress. Long-term effects can only be guessed at by comparing the BP explosion to the 1989 Exxon Valdez disaster in Prince William Sound, Alaska.

The United Houma Nation appealed to BP's Deepwater Horizon compensation fund for assistance, but BP turned them down because without federal recognition, the Houma Nation was not entitled to assert claims. I quote here the brief memo sent to the tribe:

While BP indeed processes claims from federally recognized Indian Tribes through this process, our review of your claim submission indicates that the United Houma Nation is not a federally recognized Indian Tribe entitled to assert claims pursuant to the Oil Pollution Act of 1990 ("OPA"). Therefore, we are closing your claim file with regard to this matter.[24]

The United Houma Nation has had a petition for federal recognition pending for thirty years, and its members are still waiting for an answer. Interestingly, it has been the oil and gas industry that has proven the major opposition to the tribe's petition. The lack of standing in the federal government's eyes has been a major impediment to the United Houma Nation's efforts to rebuild and save what is left of their lands.

Robichaux, who was principal chief for thirteen years—including those during which Katrina and Rita struck—was able to form a group of volunteers out of the many who came to Louisiana to help after the hurricanes. She applied for recovery grants from nonprofit organizations on behalf of the tribe, and, most important, she spoke on stations such as National Public Radio to publicize the damage caused by the BP blowout.[25] Robichaux and current principal chief, Thomas Dardar Jr., have testified before the Senate regarding the tribe's recovery efforts, the impact of their lack of federal recognition on recovery, and their future as a distinct cultural and political entity.

According to Robichaux, the recent hurricanes and the BP disaster affect the United Houma Nation on three levels: economic, because of the collapse of the fishing industry, which employs so many of the Houma men; environmental, given the collapse of the habitats of fish, shrimp, oysters, and crabs; and cultural, considering the possibility of relocation for United Houma Nation tribal members who have lived on the land for centuries. These three levels are so closely intertwined that any adverse outcome at any of the three levels would imperil the United Houma Nation's future.[26] Robichaux testified before the House Committee on Natural Resources oversight hearing:

> The relationship between the Houma People and these lands is fundamental to our existence as an Indian nation. The medicines we use to prevent illnesses and heal our sick, the places our ancestors are laid to rest, the fish, shrimp, crabs, and oysters our people harvest, our traditional stories and the language we speak are all tied to these lands inextricably. Without these lands, our culture and way of life that has been passed down generation to generation will be gone.[27]

Many of the medicinal plants used by the traiteurs, or traditional healers, are disappearing, along with the land they grow on. The palmetto leaves used to make traditional Houma baskets are harder to find now, as the trees they grow on are dying from soil erosion and saltwater intrusion. The possibility of relocation may mean the loss of the cultural activities that help define the people as Houma.

What does the future hold for the United Houma Nation? In 1998, the state of Louisiana embarked upon a multiphased plan to restore its coast at what is estimated to cost fifty billion dollars over fifty years. The mission statement of this comprehensive plan, called Coast 2050, calls for "a technically sound strategic plan to sustain coastal resources and provide an integrated multiple-use approach to ecosystem management."[28] In order to accomplish this goal, and in order to save other communities, certain coastal areas now below sea level—including many traditional Houma settlements—will not be included in the plan. Instead, they will be designated "sacrifice" or "trade-off" communities. The state of Louisiana's explanation is that these low-lying communities are too costly to protect.[29]

Because they were left out of the Coast 2050 plan, the United Houma Nation has assumed its own plans. In 2011, they took part in an effort spearheaded by America's WETLAND Foundation, along with the Terrebonne Parish government and local community agencies, placing hundreds of floating mats planted with marsh grass in the wetlands' open waters. The hope is that the grasses will put down roots, creating new land.[30]

The creation of land narratives also plays a crucial role in Houma efforts to combat the economic, environmental, and cultural effects of recent events. After the BP Deepwater Horizon blowout, the United Houma Nation partnered with the nonprofit Bridge the Gulf project on a youth media lab. Young Houma people were given video cameras, which they used to document what was happening to their homelands. They were mentored by tribal members and Bridge the Gulf volunteers, such as Dana Solet. As Solet explained, "Many times reporters will come with an agenda or story already in mind. What they want are quotes to fill in their story. What we're doing is to tell our own story, through our own eyes."[31] Volunteer mentor Bryan Parras reminded the young people that although the video camera is a tool, it can also "be used as a weapon."[32] In a brainstorming session, the young videographers came up with what they wanted to convey to outsiders, such as caution signs on the bayous that demonstrate why their parents can no longer fish as they used to. Ultimately, as Solet stated, "If we don't fight for ourselves, no one else will."[33]

The United Houma Nation, in partnership with nonprofit organizations like Bridge the Gulf and Green for All, is using open-source social media outlets, such as Facebook and YouTube, to make their situation known outside of Louisiana. In a series of brief personal videos uploaded to YouTube in 2010, Houma people discuss the damage to their homeland and what the future holds. Lora Ann Chaisson, a tribal council member, speaks of her concern for the water. "The dispersants are something new," she states. "It will be years and years before the water is safe."[34] The chemical dispersants used by BP are also a source of worry for Jamie Billiot, who lives in Dulac. She asks, "August is right around the corner. What happens if we get another hurricane here? . . . All of this will be gone. We won't be able to live here any more. Seriously." John Silver, current tribal treasurer and Dulac resident, notes that 30 percent of the nation's seafood and 30 percent of its oil and gas come from his area, but the community doesn't see the benefits. Speaking of the future, he comments, "These communities probably won't exist the way we know it today."[35]

The economic, environmental, and cultural impacts of the recent super-hurricanes and the BP Deepwater Horizon blowout have put the Houma people in a precarious situation. They receive no help from the federal government on a tribal level because of their status as a federally unrecognized tribe, and the state of Louisiana has designated 80 percent of their communities as "sacrifice" communities. Some, like Michael T. Mayheart Dardar, have contemplated relocating to higher ground.[36] The tribe has plans to buy property north of its present communities, but fundraising is necessary to accomplish this. According to Dardar, there are short-term options and long-term options. In the short term, there is adaptation to the new environment: raising houses even higher, shifting lifestyles away from a reliance on land and toward a greater involvement in the cash economy. The long-term option is fraught with tension for tribal members: relocation. The tribe has faced relocation historically, as when they were forced out of Bayou Cane, near Houma; they consequently left behind their major agricultural practices to become fishermen and trappers. Many tribal members are deeply attached to the older communities of Pointe-aux-Chenes, Dulac, and Golden Meadow, and they refuse to consider leaving. Finding a place where the nation can relocate as a whole will be problematic. Yet it is possible, if their petition for federal recognition is met with such recognition.

"Relocation" is a highly charged term in Indian Country. Historically, for Native people it has meant forced relocation by the government from homelands to other, less desirable locations. For the Houma, however, the scenario is different. They are literally losing the ground beneath their feet. Tied to their land are culture, language, subsistence, and traditional ecological knowledge. This time, relocation is a consequence of climate change (rising sea levels caused by glacial melt, storm intensification) and man-made disasters (dredging and canal building by the oil and gas industry, the BP Deepwater Horizon explosion). How will the Houma be classified? As evacuees or internally displaced peoples? As Loretta Ross points out, "The first term has no legal basis in international law while the second term is a status that affords legal rights and protections defined by human rights treaties."[37]

The United Houma Nation takes its place next to other Native nations facing relocation as a result of climate change. The Alaska Native villages of Kivalina and Shishmaref are similarly contending with coastal erosion and flooding. Over the past fifty years, Alaska has warmed at twice the rate of the national average. This contributes to the thawing of permafrost, the boundary of which will shift northward hundreds of miles by the end of the century, increasing the risk of infrastructure damage.[38] At first glance, the Alaska Native villages would appear to have little to do with the United Houma Nation in Louisiana. However, they share commonalities, such as storm surges resulting from open bodies of water. The Houma situation comes from the ever-increasing open space in the marshlands, and the Alaska Native villages' situation from disappearing seawalls and shorelines.

The self-governing Alaska Native village of Kivalina, a traditional Inupiaq community, was never intended to be a permanent village site. The Kivalina profile on the NANA Regional Corporation's website explains:

> According to elder knowledge, the original permanent settlement known as Kivalina was located on the coast of the mainland, a few miles north of Kivalliik Channel. The people of Kivalina . . . utilized the barrier reef only as seasonal hunting grounds, making camp there in warm-weather months. The first recorded "Western" history of Kivalina occurred in 1847 when a Russian naval officer mistook a seasonal hunting camp at the north end of Kivalina Lagoon—a few miles from the location of modern-day Kivalina—as a permanent settlement, the name of which he logged as "Kivualinagmut."[39]

Kivalina's first "relocation" occurred in 1905, when the Bureau of Indian Affairs mistook a seasonal hunting camp on the barrier island for a permanent settlement. The BIA built a school on the site and declared that any inhabitants from the surrounding geographical areas who did not enroll their children in the school would be imprisoned. Those from the original Kivalina settlement and other outlying communities were thus impelled to move to the barrier island.[40]

The Native village of Kivalina is at present a two-square-mile barrier island lying ten feet above sea level, surrounded by the Chukchi Sea on one side and a lagoon on the other. It lies seventy miles north of the Arctic Circle and is one thousand miles from Anchorage. Even by Alaska standards, Kivalina is classified as an "isolated community."[41] The people of Kivalina are traditional subsistence hunters, primarily of sea mammals; they are the only people in the area to hunt the bowhead whale in accordance with International Whaling Commission standards. The opportunities for employment are extremely limited—the largest employers are the school district, with nineteen employees, and the city of Kivalina, with ten.[42]

The signs of climate change in Kivalina's coastal Arctic region have been evident to government agencies since the 1970s and since even earlier to residents. The most alarming sign of change is that ice forms later and melts earlier, resulting in longer periods of time without the protection and resources provided by the sea ice.[43] As the ice melts, sea mammals the Inupiaq have hunted for centuries, such as seals, walruses, and polar bears, move out of hunting range, leaving the people without a reliable food source. And as the climate becomes warmer, insects that were not previously known in the area have arrived—as have willow trees, now considered an invasive species. The village had been protected from winter storms by a barrier of sea ice that has now melted, leaving the area exposed to a massive erosion problem.[44] Since a series of intense storms in 2004, one hundred feet of coastline have been lost because of erosion, exposing the permafrost beneath. Two years later, storms led to a protective seawall washing away, causing the village to be declared a state flood disaster area. In 2007, a severe storm led to evacuation of the village.[45] A two-day storm on November 9 and 10, 2011, further eroded the island. This storm was particularly severe, spurring a resident to stand close to the revetment wall videotaping the storm surge, the footage of which she later uploaded to YouTube. The resident, under the username midaswanify, notes in her description, "[I am] standing as close as I can to the storm surge to catch the impacts on the rock revetment seawall."[46]

Erosion has been a problem even longer than storm intensification and early ice melt from climate change. Village elder Joe Swan recalls, "This erosion started in 1952. That's when it started. Not that much, but it was eroding, slowly. But recently, it's very fast, and if you look at old pictures, the shoreline, the erosion is coming in fast."[47] An account from an 1883 exploration of the area described the island as being 1,800 feet wide, over three times what it is at present.[48] Kivalina covered fifty-four acres at the time of the first vote on relocation by village members in 1953, the results of which were a tie and, ultimately, a decision not to relocate. The issue was voted on again in 1963, with the same results. Storm intensification, flooding, thawing permafrost, and shoreline erosion continued leading up to the time of the 1992 vote for relocation. Kivalina now covers twenty-seven acres, and diminishes with every storm.

It wasn't until 1998 that the U.S. Army Corps of Engineers began the Kivalina Relocation Master Plan. That same year, residents voted to relocate to the site of Igrugaivik. In 2006, the Corps issued a finding of imminent danger, and recommended that Kivalina permanently move from its present location.[49] The Corps rejected Igrugaivik as a possible relocation site, declaring it unstable. In yet another vote, Kivalina residents settled on Kiniktuuraq, a site they had visited during hunting trips. The Corps and its contractor referred to the site in memorandums as "vulnerable to erosion" and located in a floodplain.[50] This conflicted with the people's traditional knowledge of the locale, which included no collective recollection of flooding or erosion. The disagreement has stopped relocation in its tracks, leaving residents vulnerable to the sea and without funding for elements as essential as an evacuation road.

In 2008, the Corps built a rock revetment wall, which is meant to last ten to fifteen years with proper maintenance. Unfortunately, Congress repealed the authority of the Corps to construct and maintain such structures in 2009.[51] The revetment may not survive another series of storms like those of the 2000s. Clearly, Kivalina needs to relocate, but the question is: Who will pay for it, and how? There is no government agency to oversee relocations of entire tribal communities, and there are no proactive measures in place to make sure that disasters do not strike. Help only arrives *after* disasters happen.

Kivalina city manager Janet Mitchell has indicated that the village leadership has "talked to everybody except the president of the United States. . . . We talked to Governor Parnell, Senator Stevens has been here and seen the problems we're facing. We've talked to . . . FEMA, the Corps. Nothing happens."[52] Daniel Cordalis and Dean B. Suagee point out that the United States "has a trust responsibility to tribes, which includes fiduciary obligations to tribes for the management of tribal trust lands and resources."[53] Because there is no lead entity on the matter, the trust responsibility is not being fulfilled. Village elder Enoch Adams also notes the trust responsibility of the government:

> The federal government has a trust responsibility to the tribes, and they need to enact that. The state of Alaska needs to pony up monies that they have been taking by getting resources from our land, and share it with the communities that need it the most. When you take a real close look at this, this is a human rights issue. There is racism involved. There is class warfare. There is that rural versus urban Alaska thing.[54]

As Adams implies, power and decision making on the relocation issue are being taken out of local hands and placed into the hands of various governmental agencies, with no one taking the lead.

The world might never have heard of Kivalina's predicament had it not been for the people's turn to the courts: in February 2008, the village filed suit in a U.S. district court against twenty-four fossil fuel companies for contributing to erosion through greenhouse gas emissions, and, more important, for creating a false debate on the issue of climate change.[55] In the case *Native Village of Kivalina v. ExxonMobil Corporation, et al.*, Kivalina based its complaint on claims of federal common law of public nuisance, civil conspiracy, and concert of action. One year later, the court granted the defendants' motion to dismiss. Kivalina appealed to the U.S. Court of Appeals for the Ninth Circuit, which upheld the dismissal.

As Cordalis and Suagee state, "The framework of climate change law that is emerging in the United States has not yet solidified. Rather, there are only miscellaneous federal laws that relate to climate change."[56] As a result of its novelty, Kivalina's suit brought an initial flurry of media attention, which then rapidly diminished. The most recent development of any kind in the Kivalina relocation matter is the village's petition for writ of certiorari—filed with the U.S. Supreme Court on February 25, 2013—in which Kivalina sought damages for the cost of relocation.

Such petitions are rarely granted by the nation's highest court, and they are only granted for compelling reasons. Kivalina's petition was dismissed without a hearing on May 20, 2013.

Journalists, scientists, missionaries, and other adventurers continue to make their way to Kivalina, documenting what they find in photographs and videotapes and frequently uploading these to social media outlets. The people of Kivalina are similarly documenting their land and their lives—through social media and interviews and interactions with outsiders—in an effort to disseminate information about their predicament.

Long ago, all there was here was water and sand. There was no village and no one lived here. One day a fierce storm raged. The constant roar of the furious sea sounded like thunder. The powerful waves threw tree trunks up onto the sand. The tree trunks stayed where they were. As time passed, grass and other plants grew over them. The grass captured new sand, and the hills began to form. The new land rose higher and higher. . . . That is how Shishmaref was created. . . . But someday the land will return to the way it was. It will sink back into the sea. Only the sand will remain, without houses or people, and the place will look just like it did all those many years ago.

—As told by Ardith Weyiouanna to her granddaughter Emma Bessie[57]

Ardith Weyiouanna's version of the Shishmaref creation story, like other creation stories recounted in this book, begins with water. Unlike the others, this one ends with water as well, as if the Inupiaq village of Shishmaref had never existed. "Inupiaq" means Real People, and they have long and deep ties to their coastal region and to neighboring related groups, such as the Yu'pik and Alutiiq. Together they called themselves nunaqatigiitch, or "people who are linked to each other through possession of the land."[58] Now the village is confronting what was once unthinkable: the destruction of their land and the dispersal of their community.

Like Kivalina, the Alaska Native village of Shishmaref is a federally recognized Inupiaq traditional community. It is located on a one-quarter-mile-wide and three-mile-long barrier island in the Chukchi Sea, twenty miles south of the Arctic Circle and fifty miles northeast of the Bering Strait. Toward the beginning of the twentieth century, the village became a year-round settlement upon the introduction of government-run schools and other institutions, such as a post office built in 1901. The residents continue to practice a subsistence lifestyle, using snow-mobiles and boats to reach their camps. Their primary subsistence foods, according to Luci Eningowuk's eloquent 2004 testimony before the U.S. Senate Committee on Appropriations on the subject of the relo-cation effort, "include bearded seal, walrus, fish, moose, musk-oxen, caribou, ducks, geese, ptarmigan, berries and assorted greens. . . . Our grocery store is out there, in the water and on the land."[59]

Climate change has already impacted Shishmaref residents' subsis-tence practices. Caleb Pungowiyi has observed that since the 1970s, "Alaska Natives along the coast of the Chukchi Sea have noticed sub-stantial changes in the ocean and the animals that live there."[60] Bird migrations are occurring earlier, caterpillars are emerging on bushes, and other insects previously unseen in the region are appearing as well. The tree line has moved westward into a previously treeless area. South winds have increased in summer months, bringing more rain. The sea ice that once provided a barrier for the island has materialized later in the year, leaving the island with fewer defenses against fall storms. The ice that does form is thinner, which affects the sea mammals the Inupiaq villagers rely on as a food source.[61]

Compounding the effects of the later formation of sea ice barriers, the land that undergirds Shishmaref is a "fine, silty sand highly vulnerable to erosion."[62] It sits atop permafrost, which is thawing as a result of the warmer weather. By the time of Eningowuk's 2004 Senate testimony, the north shore of the island was eroding—because of storm intensifica-tion and the lack of a sea ice barrier—at a rate of three to five feet per year. Higher rates of erosion occurred during memorable storms in 1973, 1997, 2001, and 2003. During the 1997 storm, "more than 30 feet of shoreline eroded, requiring the immediate relocation of 14 homes."[63] Erosion is also occurring from the southern lagoon side, hastening the complete erosion of the island.

In 2001, the community created the Shishmaref Erosion and Relocation Coalition, made up of the governing members of the city and Native village along with representation from the village's elder and youth councils.[64] Many consider the highly destructive twenty-four-hour storm of October 7, 2001, to have been the tipping point—in 2002, the community voted to relocate. A strategic plan for relocation was created that year, and in 2006 an inland site, Tin Creek, was approved as the destination. However, relocation has yet to occur. The U.S. Army Corps of Engineers estimates that relocation to the new site would cost $180 million. If relocation does not take place, the village has an estimated ten to fifteen years before it is completely eroded and flooded.[65]

The story of the plight of Shishmaref was circulated widely in the mid-2000s by the media. Along with being featured in Alaskan newspapers, the village was profiled on *The Oprah Winfrey Show* and in *People* magazine, the *New York Times*, and the *New Yorker*. Former vice president-turned-environmentalist Al Gore declared the residents of Shishmaref to be "the world's first climate change refugees."[66] But public interest in and knowledge of Shishmaref has fizzled out at a most crucial time. As Luci Eningowuk testified in 2004, "[O]ur situation is urgent, we are unlikely to survive until new Statutes, Regulations, or Policies can be developed and implemented. . . . But, right now, we are barely holding on, as we watch the sea eat away at everything we, and you, have built."[67]

The changing climate conditions in both Kivalina and Shishmaref have challenged the people's ability to read the ice and other weather indicators. This, in turn, creates travel hazards, resulting in snowmobiles plunging through the thin ice. As the population grows from its current (as of the publication of this book) number of 609, there is literally no land on which to build new houses for grandchildren. There is no safe place for children to play. Several generations live together in small houses, which were not built to withstand the current conditions. There are no sewage or water systems. A gallon of drinking water costs an average of seven to eight dollars. These are fourth-world living conditions; they cannot be sustained. Clarence Alexander et al., point out the irony inherent in the fact that "climate change is being experienced by many indigenous communities that have not participated in the industrial activity that is its primary cause."[68] Apart from generators, snowmobiles, and ATVs, the residents of Kivalina and Shishmaref live "off the grid."

Kivalina and Shishmaref are not the only Alaska Native villages in this predicament. In fact, 86 percent of Alaska Native villages are threatened by erosion and flooding. Of these, thirty-one villages face severe threats, while twelve have plans to relocate. How these relocation plans will proceed remains to be seen, given the large cost and the absence of a governmental entity to take the lead.

Like the United Houma Nation, whose homelands have been left out of the Coast 2050 plan and designated as "sacrifice communities," so, too, have the Alaska Native villages of Kivalina and Shishmaref seemingly been left to their own devices, sacrificed while the rest of the world continues its consumption and emission of fossil fuels and greenhouse gases. The federal recognition status of each village has not helped Kivalina or Shishmaref (other than through the construction of a revetment wall to protect against sea waves). Their federal status has not made the process of relocation any faster; on the contrary, it may have made the process more cumbersome. For all three Native communities in this case study, power relations have been constructed in such a manner that the communities are left outside the margin.

"Idle No More"

First Nations Women and Environmental Struggles

ONE DECEMBER MORNING IN 2012, my e-mail inbox exploded. My friend Hélène in Manitoba had added me to a Facebook group called Idle No More. The e-mail notifications came fast and furious, with announcements of teach-ins all across Canada regarding a proposed piece of legislation called Bill C-45. My heart sank. Without even knowing the contents of the bill, I knew it was not a good thing for First Nations people. As more e-mails came pouring in, I learned of other bills, among them Bill C-38, Bill C-27, Bill S-2, and Bill C-428. Links to videos of teach-ins, which had been uploaded to YouTube, appeared as well. Yet curiously, Canadian and American media outlets were silent. Social media was my only link to what was going on with my Canadian relatives.

The Idle No More movement began in November 2012, with four women and a Twitter hashtag heard round the world: #IdleNoMore.[1] The founders of the movement—Sylvia McAdam, a Cree lawyer and educator; Nina Wilson (Nakota and Plains Cree); Jessica Gordon (Cree and Anishinaabe); and Sheelah McLean (non-Native)—first discussed the environmental implications of Bill C-45 in a Facebook thread. To be silent about the proposed bill, they agreed, was to acquiesce; they would hence be "idle no more." The mission of McAdam and the other founders was to start a community discussion of the two huge omnibus bills—Bill C-38 (Budget Omnibus #1) and Bill C-45 (Budget Omnibus #2)—presented to the Parliament of Canada in October 2012 by Prime Minister Stephen Harper's government. The bills would drastically affect not only members of First Nations, but all Canadians. McAdam explained in a radio interview that she first began studying Bill C-45, an 450-plus-page omnibus bill, after someone tagged her in a comment about it on Facebook. Despite her legal training, she had to read it with her copy of *Black's Law Dictionary* by her side.[2]

What exactly does Bill C-45, disguised under an innocuous title— the Job and Growth Act—attempt to accomplish in its 450-plus pages? According to a summary of federal legislative amendments prepared by Laura Land, Liora Zimmerman, and Andrea Bradley, as well as information provided during teach-ins led by Sylvia McAdam and Pam Palmater, the bill changed forty-four federal laws without either proper parliamentary debate or consultation with First Nations (such consultation is required by the Constitution of Canada). Among the changes that affect First Nations are the proposed removal of fish-habitat protections and the removal of recognition of First Nations commercial fisheries. Some of the most pressing concerns, however, derive from the proposed changes to the Navigable Waters Protection Act of 1882 (now called the Navigation Protection Act), which would reduce the number of lakes requiring federal environmental assessment from 32,000 to just 97, and the number of such rivers from 2.25 million to 62. This works out to a "shocking" loss of environmental protection for 99 percent of Canadian waterways.[3] The majority of these lakes and waterways are in First Nations land or unceded territory.

The clear winners here are Prime Minister Harper's government and multinational corporations in the business of resource extraction. What immediately comes to mind are the vast corporations behind the Alberta tar sands operations and the proposed Enbridge Northern Gateway pipeline through British Columbia, which would benefit from the proposed legislation and relaxed environmental protection laws. Those on the losing end will not only be First Nations members, who will be disproportionately affected, but all Canadians. As actress and activist Tantoo Cardinal puts it, "If you drink water, you should be paying attention."[4]

During a teach-in in Alberta in December 2012, Pam Palmater explained that, according to the treaties, First Nations and settler

Canadians "live here together as treaty partners. All that is left of reserve land is 0.2 percent—it could fit on Vancouver Island."[5] She added that Bill C-45 includes an amendment to the Indian Act. This amendment "lowers the threshold for surrender of Indian reserve lands." Such a surrender "doesn't have to be approved by the cabinet." What further troubled Palmater is the First Nations Property Ownership Act, which she referred to as the Dawes Act for twenty-first-century Canada. The First Nations Property Ownership Act takes away communal lands, gives out allotments, and makes lands available for purchase by outsiders. "This act," she pointed out, "is the easiest way to get around community referendums."[6] Its objectives are to destroy First Nations communities and governments and allow resource extraction, such as the proposed tar sands pipeline. Every discussion of the act emphasizes the damage done in the United States by the Dawes Act. Over and over, speakers at teach-ins and rallies cover in detail the inevitable effects of the legislative acts on First Nations and Canadian populations. The speakers' goals are simple: to protect the waterways and land for all Canadians, and to protect indigenous sovereignty.

The first teach-in was held a week after the online conversation about Bill C-45 between McAdam, Wilson, Gordon, and McLean. It took place at a donated venue in Saskatoon, Saskatchewan, and utilized the slogan Idle No More. The Saskatoon teach-in focused on the largest of the bills, C-45, and included guest speakers, petitions, and the building of a grassroots movement in opposition to the proposed bill. Jessica Gordon set up a Facebook page (http://www.facebook.com/IdleNoMoreCommunity) in order to begin a dialogue and coordinate requests for teach-ins in other areas. Fueled by social media, the movement has grown exponentially across Canada, especially among Native youth. It has crossed the border into the United States, and has spread around the globe.

A number of events increased the social media traffic and number of grassroots supporters of the movement. On December 4, 2012, the chiefs of the Assembly of First Nations (AFN) were refused entry to the House of Commons in the Canadian capital of Ottawa, where they had intended to engage in a discussion of Bill C-45. As Lisa Charleyboy notes, news of the snub immediately spread via Facebook and Twitter, in the process gaining even more followers for the movement.[7] A national day of action had previously been designated for December 10, 2012, coinciding with Amnesty International's Human Rights Day. Rallies, protests, and teach-ins were held across Canada, spurred on by the Harper government's rebuff of the AFN chiefs. The following day, Chief Theresa Spence of the Attawapiskat First Nation began a hunger strike. It lasted forty-four days, until a meeting did take place between the AFN chiefs, the governor general, and Prime Minister Harper. Still there was no mainstream media coverage of the events.

According to documents obtained by the parent company of the *Vancouver Sun* under the Access to Information Act of 1985, Harper's government and Aboriginal Affairs and Northern Development Canada (AANDC) had never heard of the Idle No More movement as of mid-December 2012. It took an e-mail from Steve Young, an Aboriginal Affairs communications worker, to his regional director on December 12, 2012, to sound the alert. "What do you mean, 'idle no more'?" responded Atlantic Region Director Ian Gray. Young explained, "Idle No More is the rallying statement for all the First Nations protesting Harper government actions. In other words, we aren't going to sit by and take this. Since mainstream media isn't giving a lot of coverage they are using social media quite effectively . . . it's actually a great case study in grassroots use of new technology."[8] This exchange illuminates the poor relationship not only between First Nations peoples and the Harper government, but also between First Nations peoples and the mainstream media. Eight days later, on December 20, then Aboriginal Affairs minister John Duncan was given a briefing note that detailed "a potential turning point in relations between the Crown and First Nations," which would make the passing of legislative changes more difficult.[9] The government also commissioned a social media analysis. The findings had the same conclusion as Steve Young: as quoted by *Vancouver Sun* reporters Jordan Press and Michael Woods, "This was a movement the likes of which the government had never seen before."[10]

On December 14, 2012, a mere three days after Chief Spence began her hunger strike, Bill C-45 was passed by Canada's Parliament. On December 17, the protests for which the movement would become known worldwide began in shopping malls throughout Canada. What made the protests indelible was the form they took: the flash mob round dance.[11] The first occurred at the Cornwall Centre in Regina, Saskatchewan; another took place the next day at the West Edmonton Mall in Alberta. They continued all across Canada during the pre- and post-Christmas shopping seasons, eventually spilling over into the United States. Over one thousand people participated in a flash mob round dance in the east rotunda of Minnesota's Mall of America on December 29, 2012.[12] Reporter Sheila Regan of the *Twin Cities Daily Planet* interviewed an elderly woman at the round dance "who wanted to . . . show solidarity with Canadian First Nations People." The woman's concern was that if Bill C-45 became law in Canada, "it could possibly happen here."[13] By December 27, 2012, there had reportedly been over one hundred protests in Canada. The flash mobs finally garnered attention for Idle No More from the Canadian mainstream media, and, to a lesser extent, from the American media.

The Idle No More movement arrived in the Kansas City metropolitan area in December 2012, via a Facebook invitation sent to local Native organizations, tribal governments, individuals, and activists for two different flash mob round dances—one in a shopping mall on the Missouri side, and one on the Kansas side, to be held later on the same afternoon. I decided to attend the later one, as it was closer to my home. Again through Facebook, the participants were informed that this was a peaceful protest, and that we were to leave promptly and quietly if asked to do so. I arrived at the shopping mall early and purchased a small item, so that I could prove I had legitimate business there. As I walked toward the center court, I realized that I had never seen so many Indians in a shopping mall at one time before. The singers, holding hand drums, started a round dance song; we all locked arms together and began to dance. Shoppers crowded around us and hung over the second-floor railings for a better look. Some filmed the action with their cell phones. We made it through two push-ups (or verses) before an irate mall security guard shoved his way through toward one of the singers and said, "You've got to stop this now." The singer said, "Okay," and stopped, much to the security guard's surprise. The guard turned to the dancers and shouted, "All of you out of here, now!" I turned and headed for the exit near where I had parked my car. On my way, I passed two more security guards heading for the center court. I overheard one say, "There's two hundred Indians dancing and they're all riled up." In actuality, there were only about fifty of us, and no one was riled up. As I reached the exit door along with one of the singers, we heard sirens and saw nine city police SUVs pull up next to the curb. The officers paid no attention to us as we hit the farthest door and walked out into the parking lot to our cars.

By the time I arrived home, the flash mob round dance was already posted to YouTube. I also had several urgent Facebook messages telling everyone not to go to the Kansas mall, as the local police had been notified and they would be arresting people for trespassing. Not having a smartphone, I didn't get the earlier messages. There was no media coverage of the two flash mobs, even though the Facebook chatter indicated that one person had been arrested.

Two weeks later, I was in another flash mob, this one in Lawrence, Kansas, held in a public park and with a city permit. The only proviso was that we couldn't dance on the grass. Here I danced with current and former students, neighbors and friends, and colleagues. The event was covered favorably by the local paper, which sent a reporter and photographer.[14] The rest of the media was silent.

As the Idle No More movement grew, so did the pressure on Prime Minister Harper. He announced a meeting with the AFN chiefs and select First Nations leaders for Friday, January 11, 2013. On his program *The National*, CBC television journalist Peter Mansbridge responded to the impending meeting in a "Countdown to Friday" segment that tried to explain Idle No More to viewers. He began the program by stating, "It started small, but it's not that way now."[15] He posed two questions to his four invited guests, two Native and two non-Native: "Who are they?"

and "What are they looking for?" Rhetorically, these questions are formed in such a way as to be inherently divisive, especially in light of the questions Mansbridge posed later in the program: "Why is this such a divisive issue?" and "Does danger lurk?"[16] The invited guests—Wab Kinew of the University of Winnipeg; Gabrielle Scrimshaw, president of the Aboriginal Professional Association of Canada; Keith Beardsley, a journalist and former politician; and Tom Flanagan, a professor of political science at the University of Calgary—had widely divergent responses. Beardsley responded to the "Who are they?" question by outlining the various participants in the movement: 1) young people; 2) elected officials, such as the AFN chiefs and Chief Theresa Spence; and 3) indigenous and non-indigenous people around the world. Flanagan, in contrast, referred to Idle No More as having "a political cast, with the usual leftist crowd getting involved." He also called it an "aboriginal uprising."[17] When Mansbridge tried to compare Idle No More to the Arab Spring or Occupy movements, he met with resistance on all sides. Scrimshaw responded by saying that Idle No More was the result of a more focused conversation than that of Occupy. Flanagan agreed that it was different from the other movements in that this was the first time Canada had seen a spontaneous national movement fueled by the use of social media.[18]

This is just one example of the mainstream Canadian media coverage of Idle No More. Alternative publications and online news sources have also covered the movement. In the *Huffington Post Canada*, Wab Kinew wrote, "Idle No More has accomplished something all Canadians want: it has young people paying attention to politics."[19] Regarding settler Canadians, Kinew quotes Pam Palmater: "First Nations are Canadians' last, best hope of protecting the land, water, sky and plants and animals for their future generations as well."[20] It is the treaties that will ultimately secure protection of land and water for all Canadians.

After the flash mobs seemed to come to an end, Idle No More joined with an allied group, Defenders of the Land, to promote "Sovereignty Summer," comprising a "campaign of coordinated non-violent direct actions to promote Indigenous rights and environmental protection in

alliance with non-Indigenous supporters."[21] Sovereignty Summer officially launched at noon on June 21, 2013, in Queen's Park in Toronto.
The Facebook page dedicated to the campaign called for drummers and
dancers, and asked people to bring pots and pans. June 21 also happens
to be National Aboriginal Day in Canada, as well as the summer sol-
stice. Part of the Sovereignty Summer launch was dedicated to "taking
back" National Aboriginal Day as a day of "solidarity and protest."[22] The
most important aspect of Sovereignty Summer was the joint Idle
No More / Defenders of the Land "Calls for Change," which asked for:
1) the repeal of provisions of Bill C-45 affecting land, water, and First
Nations sovereignty; 2) proportional representation and consultation
on all legislation concerning collective rights and environmental
protections; 3) respect of the right of indigenous peoples to say no to
development on their territory; 4) cessation of the Canadian policy of
extinguishment of Aboriginal Title; 5) honor of the spirit and intent of
the historic treaties; and 6) a national inquiry into missing and murdered indigenous women and girls.[23]

Despite both the public rallies during the summer of 2013 and the
increased social media presence of the Idle No More/Defenders of the
Land coalition, coverage in Canadian mainstream media slipped during
this time. Idle No More was nowhere to be seen on the front pages of
newspapers or television news programs such as *The National*. At the
same time, news of rallies and strategy meetings across Canada has
reached U.S. tribes, for whom the Alberta tar sands and proposed
Keystone XL pipeline are main concerns. Idle No More and its allied
groups are becoming more focused and localized in their actions,
encouraging local autonomous groups to attend to their unique issues,
such as the Alberta tar sands, the effects of which cross the Canadian-
U.S. border, or the fracking protests in unceded Mi'kmaq territory in
New Brunswick.

As the tar sands facility in Fort McMurray, Alberta, increases its
operation, its need for equipment to process bitumen also grows. In
Idaho, twenty members of the Nez Perce Tribe, including the tribal
chairman, Silas Whitman, were arrested on August 5, 2013, for forming

a human blockade across U.S. Highway 12 near Lewiston to prevent the passage of a "megaload" of machinery bound for Fort McMurray. (At over 200 feet long and 644,000 pounds heavy, the water evaporator that makes up this particular "megaload" is but one type of machinery attempting to make its way along the narrow highway that winds through the Nez Perce-Clearwater National Forests.) Although the carrier of the megaload, Omega Morgan, indicated that they had received an oversized load permit from the Idaho Transportation Department, the U.S. Forest Service claims jurisdiction over the area. None of the entities involved consulted with the Nez Perce regarding the impact such loads would have on their lands. The tribe filed an injunction in federal court to stop the "megaloads" from operating on Highway 12. The injunction was granted in early September 2013.[24]

The hydraulic fracturing controversy in New Brunswick goes back to 2010, the year the province opened 1.4 million hectares of land, or one-seventh of the entire province, to shale-gas exploration corporations.[25] Fracking is strongly opposed in New Brunswick, and not just by the Mi'kmaq nations—Martin Lukacs's column in the *Guardian* reports that "two out of every three people in Atlantic Canada" oppose fracking.[26] This opposition stands even though the majority of resource reserves lie on Native lands.

The Mi'kmaq Elsipogtog First Nation had been peacefully demonstrating against incursion on their unceded lands by a U.S. shale-gas company, Texas's Southwestern Energy Company (SWN). On the evening of October 16, 2013, according to a timeline prepared by reporter Dylan Powell, a negotiator for the Royal Canadian Mounted Police (RCMP) presented the Elsipogtog camp with a peace offering of tobacco, after a Mi'kmaq van blocking the SWN camp was moved.[27] At six the next morning, the RCMP moved in, donning full riot gear and accompanied by K-9 units. They blocked off the highway. While drumming and singing, the Elsipogtog community and its allies broke through police lines. They were met with rubber bullets and mass arrests— including of the band chief, Aaron Sock, and a number of journalists. That afternoon, Aboriginal Peoples Television Network (APTN) reporter

Amanda Polchies (Mi'kmaq) kneels in front of a line of RCMP officers during a fracking protest in Elsipogtog, New Brunswick, Canada, on October 17, 2013. Photo by Ossie Michelin, Aboriginal Peoples Television Network (APTN).

Ossie Michelin took a photograph of Elsipogtog community member Amanda Polchies as she knelt in front of a line of RCMP holding out an eagle feather. The iconic photograph would be reprinted in newspapers across Canada, and spread throughout the world via social media.

Powell's timeline of events was confirmed by a YouTube video uploaded by Chris Sabas on October 17, 2013.[28] Sabas's video shows a number of Native women—including Amanda Polchies, whom we see being separated from the group by the RCMP—in the middle of the high-way praying and singing. The RCMP chant, "move back, move back." The women's voices seem to provide a counternarrative to the sounds of the police dogs barking. "Why did you offer the tobacco?" the women ask.

As the long day went on, police cars were set on fire; that footage was what made the evening CBC news, rather than the video shot by Chris Sabas. Just a few days later, Martin Lukacs reported, "Tens of thousands [of Canadians] have signed petitions, and many others marched along-side indigenous peoples in dozens of cities and towns."[29]

As the title of Wab Kinew's article for the *Huffington Post Canada* suggests, "Idle No More Is Not Just an 'Indian Thing.'" It is not just a Cana-dian thing, either, as demonstrated by the outpouring of support and solidarity by U.S. Native peoples, and, indeed, by indigenous peoples and allies around the world. Environmental devastation is a major concern for people of all nations, especially considering that the Alberta tar sands are positioned to be the next great environmental debacle of our time.

The Idle No More movement coincides with increased resource extraction in Canada, most of it in the north and much of it on First Nations land. Canada is in the process of becoming crisscrossed with a network of pipelines, which would potentially move crude tar sands from Fort McMurray, Alberta, to a refinery in the east. The sands would then move to the United States via the Keystone XL pipeline, and on to China, via the Enbridge Northern Gateway through British Columbia. As Canada establishes itself as an oil-producing nation alongside its long-standing ventures in mining and forestry, opposition by First Nations and everyday Canadians grows. In an interview with Occupy

Radio LDN in London, Sylvia McAdam noted that the tar sands have now grown to encompass an area the size of France. She also described the presence of new and bizarre cancers in the surrounding areas, and the fact that migratory birds are not returning.[30] The tar sands are adjacent to the Athabasca Chipewyan and Mikisew Cree First Nations, members of which, like those of other First Nations, have witnessed the extraction of vast resources from their lands. Yet they receive nothing in return.

The power of four women and a Twitter hashtag to spark a grassroots movement cannot be overestimated. The Canadian mainstream media has tried to ignore these women or cast them as political leftists, and has instead picked out (male) "leaders." However, the community website, www.IdleNoMore.ca, insists that this is a grassroots community movement with no leaders. An examination of the website demonstrates just that—anyone can join the movement or upload videos, articles, pictures, and announcements. Other social media platforms, especially Twitter, have been increasingly important as a source of information in northern communities, where Internet access is limited.

In her television interview, Tantoo Cardinal characterized the period leading up to the Idle No More movement as "smoldering."[31] The omnibus bills were tinder for the smoldering fire, causing the rise of a social movement with global implications. Idle No More is not just an Indian thing, not just a Canadian thing.

INTRODUCTION

1. Throughout this book, I use the terms "Indian," "American Indian," "Native American," and "Native" interchangeably to refer to the indigenous peoples of what is now the United States, as is common practice among many of us. In a Canadian context, I use "First Nations," "aboriginal," or "Native." Wherever possible, I use the names of individual tribal nations.

2. Hugh Prince, *Wetlands of the American Midwest: A Historical Geography of Changing Attitudes* (Chicago, IL, and London: University of Chicago Press, 1997), 5.

3. Baker University. http://www.bakeru.edu/wetlands/species-lists.

4. The land transfer of area wetlands to Baker University is part of a series of complex transactions under federal law; what I present here is simplified.

5. Such accounts are well known to Haskell students, alumni, and descendants of alumni. See http://www.savethewetlands.org/docs/wpo.htm. A wetlands scene of escape from an institution much like Haskell appears in the film *The Only Good Indian*, directed by Kevin Willmott (TLC Films, Lawrence, KS, 2009).

6. Keith Basso, *Wisdom Sits in Places: Landscape and Language Among the Western Apache* (Albuquerque: University of New Mexico Press, 1995), 7. The term "native space" comes from Lisa Brooks's excellent monograph *The Common Pot: The Recovery of Native Space in the Northeast* (Minneapolis: University of Minnesota Press, 2008).

7. Sondra Van Meter McCoy and Jan Hults, *1001 Kansas Place Names* (Lawrence: University of Kansas Press, 1989), 203.

8. The district court ruling has not gone unnoticed or unremarked by the Native community in Lawrence. While I was attending a retirement party for a friend at the Haskell Health Clinic, I overheard two Native women discussing the ruling and surplus land transfers, which, collectively, did not just give away the wetlands to Baker, but also gave twenty acres of wetlands to the University of Kansas and gave the land where Broken Arrow Elementary School is now located.

9. The term "narrated place-worlds" comes from Basso, *Wisdom Sits in Places*, 32.

10. Renya K. Ramirez has theorized that these and other gatherings are "'hubs' . . . that bridge tribal differences." See Ramirez, *Native Hubs: Culture, Community, and Belonging in Silicon Valley and Beyond* (Durham, NC: Duke University Press, 2007), 8. Nicholas G. Rosenthal and Joan Weibel-Orlando have both explored the

federal relocation program and the building of the Los Angeles Indian community. See Rosenthal, *Reimagining Indian Country: Native American Migration and Identity in Twentieth-Century Los Angeles* (Chapel Hill: University of North Carolina Press, 2012), and Weibel-Orlando, *Indian Country, L.A.: Maintaining Ethnic Community in Complex Society* (Urbana: University of Illinois Press, 1991). Kent MacKenzie's recently restored and commercially released film *The Exiles* (1961; Los Angeles, CA: Milestone Films, 2008) focuses on characters relocated to Los Angeles from reservations in the Southwest under the federal relocation program.

11. The term "recognition" is receiving wider critical attention, even as federally recognized tribes themselves often oppose petitions for federal recognition by other Native communities. Glen Sean Coulthard notes that the term itself shapes current debates over indigeneity, politics, and sovereignty. See Glen Sean Coulthard, *Red Skin, White Masks: Rejecting the Colonial Politics of Recognition* (Minneapolis: University of Minnesota Press, 2014).

12. See the Native American and Indigenous Studies Association, http://www.naisa.org.

13. See Jace Weaver's *That the People Might Live: Native American Literatures and Native American Communities* (New York: Oxford University Press, 1997); Craig Womack's *Red on Red: Native American Literary Separatism* (Minneapolis: University of Minnesota Press, 1999); and Daniel Heath Justice's *Our Fire Survives the Storm: A Cherokee Literary History* (Minneapolis: University of Minnesota Press, 2005). Other scholarly books working toward linking Native studies with postcolonialism include Jodi A. Byrd, *The Transit of Empire: Indigenous Critiques of Colonialism* (Minneapolis: University of Minnesota Press, 2011); with women and gender, Shari M. Huhndorf, *Mapping the Americas: The Transnational Politics of Contemporary Native Culture* (Ithaca, NY: Cornell University Press, 2009); with law, Justin Richland, *Arguing with Tradition: The Language of Law in Hopi Tribal Court* (Chicago, IL: University of Chicago Press, 2008); and with ecocriticism, Joni Adamson, *American Indian Literature, Environmental Justice, and Ecocriticism: The Middle Place* (Tucson: University of Arizona Press, 2001).

14. Huhndorf, *Mapping the Americas*, 4.

15. Sue-Ellen Jacobs, Wesley Thomas, and Sabine Lang, eds., "Introduction" in *Two Spirit People: Native American Gender Identity, Sexuality, and Spirituality* (Urbana and London: University of Illinois Press, 1997), 2.

16. Joni Adamson and Scott Slovic, "The Shoulders We Stand On: An Introduction to Ethnicity and Ecocriticism," *MELUS: Multi-Ethnic Literature of the United States* 34.2 (2009): 6.

17. Maureen Konkle, *Writing Indian Nations: Native Intellectuals and the Politics of Historiography, 1827–1863* (Chapel Hill: University of North Carolina Press, 2004), 2.

18. Diné Natural Law or Nahasdzáán dóó Yádiłhił Bitsą́ądęę Beenahaz'áanii, Title 1, ch. 1, §5, Navajo Nation Code (2002). http://www.navajocourts.org/dine.htm.

19. "Resolution of the Navajo Nation Council, Amending Title 1 of the Navajo Nation Code to Recognize the Fundamental Laws of the Diné." http://www.navajocourts.org/resolutions.htm.

20. Ibid.

21. James M. Grijalva, *Closing the Circle: Environmental Justice in Indian Country* (Durham, NC: Carolina Academic Press, 2008), 11.

22. "The Crying Indian—full commercial—Keep America Beautiful." April 22 (Earth Day), 1971. YouTube video, 1:00. Posted by coffeekid99. https://www.youtube.com/watch?v=j7OHG7tHrNM.

23. Cody (April 3, 1904–January 4, 1999), whose birth name was Espera Oscar de Corti, was born to Sicilian immigrant parents in southwestern Louisiana.

24. Margaret Noori, "Beshaabiiag G'Gikenmaaigowag: Comets of Knowledge," in *Centering Anishinaabeg Studies: Understanding the World Through Stories*, ed. Jill Doerfler, Niigaanwewidam James Sinclair, and Heidi Kiiwetinepinesiik Stark (East Lansing: Michigan State University Press, 2013), 36.

25. Ibid.

26. Byrd, *The Transit of Empire*, xiii.

27. Basso, *Wisdom Sits in Places*, 32.

28. Esther G. Belin, "Directional Memory," in *From the Belly of My Beauty* (Tucson: University of Arizona Press, 1999), 9.

29. *Cobell v. Salazar, et al.* was a class action suit brought by lead plaintiff Elouise Pepion Cobell (Blackfeet) against the U.S. Department of the Interior and the U.S. Department of the Treasury on June 10, 1996, in the U.S. District Court for the District of Columbia, case 1:96CV01285. The thrust of the lawsuit rested on the defendants' breach of trust responsibilities to holders of IIM, or Individual Indian Money, accounts. IIM accounts are set up for individual Indians whose land is being held in trust for them by U.S. governmental departments. When such trust lands are leased out for grazing or oil exploration, the lease money is then to be deposited in these IIM accounts, with full account records and regular payment to the account holder. In *Cobell*, the plaintiffs argued that gross mismanagement of funds had taken place. Some IIM accounts and trust lands date back to the allotment era, roughly 1887 to 1934; the practice was never intended to be permanent. On December 8, 2009, the U.S. government announced that a settlement had been reached. The following year, Congress passed the Claims Resolution Act of 2010, which funded the $3.4 billion settlement, fourteen years after the original class action lawsuit had been filed. For additional information, see the Cobell Trust website: http://www.indiantrust.com.

30. Jace Weaver, *Other Words: American Indian Literature, Law and Culture* (Norman: University of Oklahoma Press, 2001), ix.

31. According to *Cohen's Handbook of Federal Indian Law*, §3.04 (2007), Section 1151's definition of "Indian Country" applies in the context of both civil and criminal law.

32. Joni Seager, "Noticing Gender (or Not) in Disasters," in *The Women of Katrina: How Gender, Race, and Class Matter in an American Disaster*, ed. Emmanuel David and Elaine Enarson (Nashville, TN: Vanderbilt University, 2012), 8.

33. Wendy Harcourt and Arturo Escobar, *Women and the Politics of Place* (Bloomfield, CT: Kumarian Press, 2005), 5.

34. Mary Helen Washington, "Disturbing the Peace: What Happens to American Studies If You Put African American Studies at the Center?: Presidential Address to the American Studies Association, October 29, 1997." *American Quarterly* 50.1 (Mar. 1998): 1–23.

35. Huhndorf, 3.

36. Elizabeth Cook-Lynn, *Why I Can't Read Wallace Stegner and Other Essays: A Tribal Voice* (Madison: University of Wisconsin Press, 1996), 40.

37. My retelling of these two traditional narratives is based on Basil Johnston's *The Manitous: The Spiritual World of the Ojibways* (New York: HarperCollins Publishers, 1995).

38. In addition to appearing in the Ojibwe creation story, Sky Woman also figures prominently in Haudenosaunee traditions. Lise Erdrich's short story "Corn Is Number One" is one example of a retelling of the Sky Woman narrative. Sky Woman also figures in contemporary mystery novels, children's books, indigenous art, and experimental film. Similarly, Nanaboozhoo has his own cycle of traditional stories, which have been collected by ethnologists, retold in children's picture books, and featured in a Marvel comic book. Nanaboozhoo's stories even have a Facebook page: http://www.facebook.com/pages/Nanabozho/110902358934383.

39. Nanaboozhoo is a figure from Ojibwe cosmology (as well other culturally and linguistically related tribes). This particular spelling comes from Basil Johnston's *The Manitous* and his *Ojibway Heritage* (Lincoln and London: University of Nebraska Press, First Bison Book Printing, 1990); as well as Edward Benton-Banai, *The Mishomis Book: The Voice of the Ojibway* (Hayward, WI: Indian Country Communications, 1988), and Victor Barnouw, *Wisconsin Chippewa Myths and Tales* (Madison: University of Wisconsin Press, 1977).

40. Noori, "Beshaabiiag G'Gikenmaaigowag," 36.

41. Taiaiake Alfred, *Wasáse: Indigenous Pathways of Action and Freedom* (Peterborough, ON: Broadview Press, 2005), 35.

CHAPTER ONE

1. Jeannette Armstrong, "Kwtlakin? What Is Your Place?," in *What Is Your Place? Indigeneity and Immigration in Canada*, ed. Hartmut Lutz (Augsburg, Germany: Wissner-Verlag, 2007), 30.

2. Ibid.

3. Leslie Marmon Silko, *Yellow Woman and a Beauty of the Spirit* (New York: Simon & Schuster, 1996), 58.

4. Cherokee Nation, *The Constitution and Laws of the Cherokee Nation: Passed at Tah-Le-Quah, Cherokee Nation, 1839* (Wilmington, DE: Scholarly Resources, Inc., 1975) 5, 15.

5. Sharri Clark, "Representing Native Identity: The Trail of Tears and the Cherokee Heritage Center in Oklahoma," *Cultural Survival Quarterly* 21.2 (1997): 36.

6. Cherokee Heritage Center. http://www.cherokeeheritage.org.

7. *Trail of Tears Exhibit*, Cherokee Heritage Center, Park Hill, Oklahoma. This oral history was recorded in the late 1930s by Grant Foreman under the auspices of the Works Progress Administration, for the Indian-Pioneer Historical Collection. Neguin walked the Trail at the age of three.

8. *Trail of Tears Exhibit*.

9. Theda Perdue and Michael D. Green refer to "nunna dual tsuny" as "a rough translation" of the term "Trail of Tears," in *The Cherokee Nation and the Trail of Tears* (New York: Viking, 2007), xiv.

10. Betty Booth Donohue, personal communication, May 17, 2013.

11. Carolyn Ross Johnston, *Cherokee Women in Crisis: Trail of Tears, Civil War, and Allotment, 1838–1907* (Tuscaloosa: University of Alabama Press, 2003), 72.

12. Barbara Duncan, *Living Stories of the Cherokee* (Chapel Hill: University of North Carolina Press, 1998), 13.

13. Quoted in Duncan, *Living Stories*, 142.

14. Vicki Rozema, *Voices from the Trail of Tears* (Winston-Salem, NC: John F. Blair, Publisher, 2003), xv.

15. Arnold Krupat, "Representing Cherokee Dispossession," *Studies in American Indian Literatures* 17.1 (2005): 21.

16. Amy Lonetree, *Decolonizing Museums: Representing Native America in National and Tribal Museums* (Chapel Hill: University of North Carolina Press, 2012), 26.

17. Cherokee Historical Association. http://www.cherokeeadventure.com.

18. "Trail of Tears" (National Park Service, 2012), DVD. http://www.nps.gov/trte/photosmultimedia/dvd.htm.

19. What was to become the Prairie Band Potawatomi tribe, for example, was forcibly marched—on what they call the Trail of Death—some 660 miles, from Plymouth, Indiana, to Osawatomie, Kansas, from September 4 to November 4, 1838.

20. Perdue and Green, *Cherokee Nation*, xiv.

21. Konkle, *Writing Indian Nations*, 42.

22. See, for example, Robert J. Conley's *Real People* series including *The Peace Chief: A Novel of the Real People* (New York: St. Martin's Press, 1998), *The Dark Way* (Norman: University of Oklahoma Press, 2000), *The Way of the Priests* (Norman: University of Oklahoma Press), *The White Path* (Norman: University of Oklahoma Press, 2000), and *Sequoyah: A Novel of the Real People* (Norman: University of Oklahoma Press, 2002); and Blake Hausman's *Riding the Trail of Tears* (Lincoln, NE: Bison Books, 2011).

23. Cherokee author Robert J. Conley is a notable exception.

24. This version is based on James Mooney's account in *Myths of the Cherokee* (Washington, D.C.: Smithsonian Institution, Bureau of American Ethnology, 1900), 239. Other versions appear in Perdue and Green, *Cherokee Nation*, 1; Christopher B. Teuton, *Deep Waters: The Textual Continuum in American Indian Literature* (Lincoln: University of Nebraska Press, 2010), xi–xii; and Duncan, *Living Stories of the Cherokee*, 40–43.

25. Perdue and Green, *Cherokee Nation*, 4.

26. Heath Justice, *Our Fire Survives the Storm*, 197.

27. Duncan, *Living Stories of the Cherokee*, 8.

28. Jennifer Andrews, "A Conversation with Diane Glancy," *American Indian Quarterly* 26.4 (2002): 649.

29. Diane Glancy, *Pushing the Bear: A Novel of the Trail of Tears* (San Diego, CA: Harcourt, Inc., 1996). 3.

30. Ibid., 4.

31. Chadwick Allen, "Postcolonial Theory and the Discourse of Treaties," *American Quarterly* 52.1 (2000): 79.

32. Glancy, *Pushing the Bear: A Novel of the Trail of Tears*, 4.

33. Ibid., 3–4.

34. Clearly, Glancy has done her research for this pair of novels.

35. Ibid., 14.

36. Ibid., 13–14.

37. Ibid., 61.

38. Ibid., 87.

39. Ibid., 125–26.

40. Ibid., 124–25.

41. Ibid., 167.

42. Allen, "Postcolonial Theory," 80.

43. Jace Weaver, "Notes from a Miner's Canary: Natives and Environmental Justice," in *Notes from a Miner's Canary: Essays on the State of Native America* (Albuquerque: University of New Mexico Press, 2010), 39.

44. Glancy, *Pushing the Bear: A Novel of the Trail of Tears,* 144.

45. Ibid., 153.

46. Ibid.

47. Ibid., 108.

48. Diane Glancy, *Pushing the Bear: After the Trail of Tears* (Norman: University of Oklahoma Press, 2009), 14–15.

49. Ibid., 25.

50. Ibid., 59.

51. Ibid., 81.

52. Ibid., 158.

53. Ibid., 184.

54. "Grandma Margaret's Long Walk Story" is told entirely in the Navajo language. YouTube video, 7:48. Posted March 3, 2009, by daybreakwarrior. https://www.youtube.com/watch?v=d85Q1U_f-l4. It complements Luci Tapahonso's poem, "In 1864," in *Sáanii Dahataał: The Women Are Singing* (Tucson: University of Arizona Press, 1993), 7.

55. Tapahonso, "In 1864," 7.

56. "Grandma Margaret's Long Walk Story."

57. Bosque Redondo Memorial. http://www.bosqueredondomemorial.com/memorial.htm.

58. Ibid., "Welcome to the Bosque Redondo Memorial." http://www.bosqueredondomemorial.com/.

59. Lonetree, 26.

60. Robert Siegel and Melissa Block, "Profile: Remembering the Navajo Long Walk," *All Things Considered,* National Public Radio, June 14, 2005.

CHAPTER TWO

1. In this chapter, I use the terms "Ojibwe," "Anishinaabe(g)," and "Chippewa" interchangeably, as they all refer to the same peoples. Chippewa is a historical term, and it remains in the names of the Turtle Mountain Band of Chippewa Indians and the Minnesota Chippewa Tribe. Similarly, I use "Indian," "Native," and "Native American" interchangeably, as there is no consensus among Native people regarding a preferred term. The term "Ojibwemowin" refers to the Ojibwe language; "Anishinaabemowin" refers to Ojibwe, Odawa, or Potawatomi languages, all of which belong to the Algonquian language family, or, alternatively, to an "Indian" language.

2. Louise Erdrich, *Books and Islands in Ojibwe Country* (Washington, D.C.: National Geographic Society, 2003), n.p., map.

3. Erdrich first uses this Ojibwe term in the singular form in *Four Souls* (New York: HarperCollins, 2004). In relating the story of Fleur's mother, she writes, "[W]hat happened that night gave slender hope on the reservation land the old ones called ishkonigan, leftover, scraps so poor even the greediest would cast these bits aside" (48). The term also appears in *The Ojibwe People's Dictionary*, http://ojibwe.lib.umn.edu.

4. Here I rely on Anne McClintock's questioning of the term "postcolonial." She explains, "[T]he term 'post-colonialism' marks history as a series of stages along an epochal road from 'the pre-colonial,' to 'the colonial,' to 'the post-colonial'—an unbidden, if disavowed, commitment to linear time and the idea of development." The idea of development was and is central to the U.S. government's American Indian policy and law. Anne McClintock, "The Angel of Progress: Pitfalls of the Term 'Post-Colonial,'" *Social Text* 31/32 (1992): 85–86.

5. Jace Weaver, "Splitting the Earth: First Utterances and Pluralist Separatism," in *American Indian Literary Nationalism*, ed. Weaver, Craig Womack, and Robert Warrior (Albuquerque: University of New Mexico Press, 2005), 64.

6. Brenda J. Child provides an interesting account of contemporary memory and the Ojibwe migration story in *Holding Our World Together: Ojibwe Women and the Survival of Community* (New York: Viking Press, 2012), xvii, xxvii. This book also contains maps of Ojibwe lands.

7. Nancy J. Peterson argues that the Allotment Act functions as an "absent presence" in *Tracks*. She writes, "The documentary history of dispossession that the novel uses and resists functions as an absent presence; the text acknowledges the way in which this historical script has impinged on the Anishinabeg, but opposes allowing this history to function as the only story that can be told." Peterson, "History, Postmodernism, and Louise Erdrich's *Tracks*," *PMLA* 109 (1994): 987.

8. Louise Erdrich, *Love Medicine*, expanded ed. (New York: HarperCollins Publishers, 1993), 11.

9. See, for example, Peterson's "History, Postmodernism, and Louise Erdrich's *Tracks*," 982–84; Julie Maristuen-Rodakowski's "The Turtle Mountain Reservation in North Dakota: Its History as Depicted in Louise Erdrich's *Love Medicine* and *The Beet Queen*," *American Indian Culture and Research Journal* 12 (1988): 33–48; and Gregory S. Camp's "Working Out Their Own Salvation: The Allotment of Land in Severalty and the Turtle Mountain Chippewa Band, 1870–1920," *American Indian Culture and Research Journal* 14 (1990): 19–38.

10. Jean Strouse, "In the Heart of the Heartland," *New York Times Book Review*, October 2, 1998.

11. Leslie Marmon Silko, "Here's an Odd Artifact for the Fairy-Tale Shelf," review of *The Beet Queen* by Louise Erdrich, *Impact/Albuquerque Journal*, October 8, 1986. Silko's review was later reprinted under the same title in *Studies in American Indian Literatures* 10 (1986): 177–84.

12. Holly Youngbear-Tibbetts, "Without Due Process: The Alienation of Individual Trust Allotments of the White Earth Anishinaabeg," *American Indian Culture and Research Journal* 15.2 (1991): 93–138. Youngbear-Tibbetts's account remains the most comprehensive social and legal history of the allotment swindles on the White Earth Reservation. See also Melissa L. Meyer's epilogue to her monograph *The White Earth Tragedy: Ethnicity and Dispossession at a Minnesota Anishinaabe Reservation, 1889–1920* (Lincoln: University of Nebraska Press, 1994), 229–35.

13. Louise Erdrich and Michael Dorris, "Who Owns the Land?," *New York Times Magazine*, September 4, 1998, 32.

14. Erdrich has engaged with political controversies on more than one occasion. There was, for instance, her 2000 *New York Times* op-ed urging clemency for Leonard Peltier, a Native American activist and American Indian Movement member whose conviction for the 1975 murders of two FBI agents on South Dakota's Pine Ridge Reservation has been the subject of ongoing controversy. More recently, her op-ed "Rape on the Reservation" drew attention to pending legislation on violence against women. "Rape on the Reservation" was printed just as her latest novel, the National Book Award–winning *The Round House*, was released; the novel centers on jurisdictional lines and sexual violence perpetrated against Native women by non-Native men. See "A Time for Human Rights on Native Ground," *New York Times*, December 29, 2000; and "Rape on the Reservation," *New York Times*, February 26, 2013.

15. Wilcomb E. Washburn, *The Assault on Indian Tribalism: The General Allotment Law (Dawes Act) of 1887* (Philadelphia, PA: J. B. Lippincott Company, 1975), 6.

16. For a discussion of Dawes, see Washburn, *The Assault on Indian Tribalism*, 25.

17. Washburn, *The Assault on Indian Tribalism*, 6.

18. Ibid., 39.

19. For a more detailed analysis of the General Allotment Act and its offshoot legislation pertaining to White Earth Reservation, see Melissa L. Meyer, *The White Earth* Tragedy, and Richard H. Weil, "Destroying a Homeland: White Earth, Minnesota," *American Indian Culture and Research Journal* 13.2 (1989): 77–78, 81.

20. D. S. Otis, *The Dawes Act and the Allotment of Indian Lands* (Norman: University of Oklahoma Press, 1973), 83.

21. Louise Erdrich, *Tracks* (New York: Harper & Row,1988), 2.

22. Susan Stanford Friedman, "Identity Politics, Syncretism, Catholicism, and Anishinabe Religion in Louise Erdrich's *Tracks,*" *Religion and Literature* 26 (1994): 107–33.

23. Erdrich, *Tracks*, 178.

24. Ibid., 32.

25. Ibid., 13.

26. Ibid., 14, 15.

27. Ibid., 38.

28. Ibid., 39.

29. Ibid., 39.

30. Ibid., 15.

31. Ibid., 11.

32. Ibid., 11.

33. Ibid., 175.

34. Ibid., 2.

35. Ibid., 2.

36. Ibid., 8.

37. Ibid., 9.

38. Ibid., 175.

39. Ibid., 173.

40. Ibid., 173.

41. Ibid., 172–73.

42. G. Thomas Couser, "Tracing the Trickster: Nanapush, Ojibwe Oral Tradition, and *Tracks,*" in *Approaches to Teaching Louise Erdrich*, ed. Greg Sarris, Connie A. Jacobs, and James R. Giles (New York: The Modern Language Association of America, 2004), 61–62.

43. Erdrich, *Tracks*, 173–74.

44. Lawrence W. Gross, "The Trickster and World Maintenance: An Anishinaabe

Reading of Louise Erdrich's *Tracks*," *Studies in American Indian Literatures* 17.3 (Fall 2005): 49.

45. Erdrich, *Tracks*, 174.

46. In the endnotes to *The Last Report on the Miracles at Little No Horse* (New York: HarperCollins Publishers, 2001), Erdrich takes care to state that "the reservation depicted in this and in all my novels is an imagined place . . . similar to many Ojibwe reservations" (357).

47. Erdrich, *Tracks*, 174.

48. See Victoria Brehm's "The Metamorphoses of an Ojibwa *Manido*," *American Literature* 68.4 (1996): 677–706, for an interesting account of traditional stories of Misshepeshu as he relates to Erdrich's work.

49. Erdrich, *Tracks*, 176.

50. Ibid., 33, 214.

51. Ibid., 220.

52. Ibid., 223.

53. Louise Erdrich, *Four Souls* (New York: HarperCollins Publishers, 2004), 79.

54. Ibid., 79.

55. Erdrich, *The Last Report*, 106.

56. Erdrich, *Four Souls*, 23.

57. Erdrich, *The Last Report*, 106.

58. Erdrich, *Four Souls*, 6.

59. Ibid., 24.

60. Ibid., 5.

61. Ibid., 4–5.

62. Ibid., 11.

63. Ibid., 5.

64. Ibid., 7.

65. Erdrich, *Tracks*, 223.

66. Ibid., 196.

67. Ibid., 33; Erdrich, *The Bingo Palace*, 148.

68. Erdrich, *The Bingo Palace*, 5.

69. Ibid., 200.

70. Ibid., 133.

71. Ibid., 219.

72. Erdrich, *Four Souls*, 210.

CHAPTER THREE

1. Michael Lawson, *Dammed Indians: The Pick-Sloan Plan and the Missouri River Sioux, 1944–1980* (Norman: University of Oklahoma Press, 1982), xix.

2. Linda Hogan, *Solar Storms* (New York: Simon & Schuster, 1995), 26.

3. "Fat-Eaters" is a fictional name that some critics have ascribed to the Inuit. See Jim Tarter, "'Dreams of Earth': Place, Multiethnicity, and Environmental Justice in Linda Hogan's *Solar Storms*," in *Reading Under the Sign of Nature: New Essays in Ecocriticism*, ed. John Tallmadge and Henry Harrington (Salt Lake City: University of Utah Press, 2000), 129.

4. Brad Johnson, "Western Voices Interview with Linda Hogan," March 2, 1998. http://www.centerwest.org/voices/Hogan-interview.htm.

5. Laura Virginia Castor, "Claiming Place in Wor(l)ds: Linda Hogan's *Solar Storms*," *MELUS* 31.2 (2006): 159.

6. Hogan, *Solar Storms*, front matter.

7. Castor, "Claiming Place in Wor(l)ds ," 158.

8. "An Interview with Linda Hogan," *Missouri Review* 17 (1994): 122.

9. Kelli Lyon Johnson, "Writing Deeper Maps: Mapmaking, Local Indigenous Knowledges, and Literary Nationalism in Native Women's Writing," *Studies in American Indian Literatures* 19.4 (2007): 114. See Elizabeth Cook-Lynn, "A Mixed-Blood, Tribeless Voice in American Indian Literatures: Michael Dorris," in *Anti-Indianism in Modern America: A Voice from Tatekeya's Earth* (Urbana: University of Illinois Press, 2001), 72–90.

10. André Picard, "James Bay II," *Amicus Journal* (Fall 1990): 16.

11. Quoted in Boyce Richardson, *Strangers Devour the Land* (White River Junction, VT: Chelsea Green Publishing Co., 1991), 84.

12. Picard, "James Bay II," 10–16.

13. Ibid., 10.

14. Ibid., 12.

15. Quoted in Picard, "James Bay II," 14.

16. Hogan, *Solar Storms*, 21.

17. The name of the village harkens back to the story of Eve's creation out of one of Adam's ribs, as well as the "broken pact" in the Garden of Eden.

18. Hogan, *Solar Storms*, 25.

19. Ibid., 89.

20. Ibid., 35.

21. Ibid., 37.

22. Ibid., 38–39.

23. It should be remembered that Hogan has created a fictional tribe, and a fictional creation story, in *Solar Storms*.

24. Hogan, *Solar Storms*, 238–39.

25. Hogan, 123.

26. R. M. Baxter, "Environmental Effects of Dams and Impoundments," *Annual Review of Ecology and Systematics* 8 (1977): 256.

27. Hogan, *Solar Storms*, 170.

28. Ibid., 170.

29. T. Christine Jespersen, "Unmapping Adventure: Sewing Resistance in Linda Hogan's *Solar Storms*," *Western American Literature* 45.3 (2010): 276.

30. This calls to mind early twentieth-century texts such as Eric Sevareid's *Canoeing with the Cree* (1930), which depicts a journey from Minneapolis to the Hudson Bay.

31. Hogan, *Solar Storms*, 225.

32. Ibid., 226.

33. Ibid., 226. This assumes, of course, that the Beautiful People are "conquered people." Some, like Tulik and his family and Miss Nett, are not. The phrase "survive like a people" is reminiscent of Nanapush's comment in Louise Erdrich's *Four Souls*: "This scrap of earth. . . . We've got this and as long as we can hold on to it we will be some sort of people" (210).

34. Hogan, *Solar Storms*, 177.

35. Ibid., 231.

36. Ibid., 251.

37. Ibid., 330.

38. The phrase is Donald Worster's—it is the title of the second chapter of *Rivers of Empire: Water, Aridity, and the Growth of the American West* (New York: Oxford University Press, 1992).

39. Elizabeth Cook-Lynn, *From the River's Edge* (New York: Arcade Publishing, 1991), 3.

40. Worster, *Rivers of Empire*, 267.

41. Lawson, *Dammed Indians*, 28, 29.

42. Ibid., 29.

43. Ibid., 45.

44. Scott Hopley and Susan Ross, "Aboriginal Claims to Water Rights Grounded in the Principle Ad Medium Filum Aquae, Riparian Rights and the Winters

Doctrine," *Journal of Environmental Law & Practice* 19 (2009): 225, 260; N. Bruce Duthu, *American Indians and the Law* (New York: Penguin Books, 2008), 105–6.

45. Lawson, *Damned Indians*, 79.

46. Ibid., 183.

47. Cook-Lynn, vii–viii. This passage was also included as a prose poem in Cook-Lynn's mixed-genre book *Then Badger Said This* (Fairfield, WA: Ye Galleon Press, 1983).

48. Elizabeth Cook-Lynn, "Question on *From the River's Edge*," e-mail to author, May 12, 2013.

49. Elizabeth Cook-Lynn, *Aurelia: A Crow Creek Trilogy* (Niwot: University of Colorado Press, 1999), 420.

50. Elizabeth Cook-Lynn, "Cosmopolitanism, Nationalism, the Third World, and First Nation Sovereignty," in *Why I Can't Read Wallace Stegner and Other Essays: A Tribal Voice*, 88.

51. Cook-Lynn, *From the River's Edge*, 71.

52. Ibid., 47–48.

53. Ibid., 48.

54. Ibid., 71.

55. Joseph Bruchac, *Survival This Way: Interviews with American Indian Poets* (Tucson: University of Arizona Press, 1987), 67.

56. Cook-Lynn, *From the River's Edge*, 136.

57. Ibid., 63. "Dakotapi" is the plural form of "Dakotah."

58. Ibid., 137.

59. Ibid., 42–43.

60. Ibid., 138.

61. *Mni Sose (aka Missouri River)*, directed by Carol Burns (Kansas City, KS, 2010), DVD.

62. Ibid.

63. Craig Howe and Kim Tall Bear, eds., *This Stretch of the River: Lakota, Dakotah, and Nakota Responses to the Lewis and Clark Expedition and Bicentennial* (Sioux Falls, SD: Oak Lake Writers' Society & Pine Hill Press, 2006), 98.

64. Ibid., 98.

CHAPTER FOUR

1. United Houma Nation. http://www.unitedhoumanation.org.

2. Ibid.

3. Ivor Van Heerden and Mike Bryan, *The Storm: What Went Wrong and Why During Hurricane Katrina—The Inside Story from One Louisiana Scientist* (New York: Viking, 2006), 153, 160.

4. Ibid., 153.

5. Greg Bowman and Janel Curry-Roper's *The Houma People of Louisiana: A Story of Indian Survival* remains the most comprehensive history of the Houma Nation (Houma, LA: The United Houma Nation, 1982), 5. The story of the United Houma Nation and coastal southeastern Louisiana is literally and figuratively one of shifting ground. The Houma people first entered the European written record through the journal of French explorer René-Robert Cavelier, sieur de La Salle. In March 1682, La Salle noted the presence of their nearby village while traveling up the Mississippi River. Chevalier de Tonti and Pierre LeMoyne d'Iberville visited the Houma village near present-day West Feliciana Parish in 1686 and 1699, respectively, cementing an alliance between the Houma and the French that would last for almost eighty years. The Houma were intended to serve as a buffer between English-allied tribes and the French settlements. Intertribal hostilities encouraged by the colonial powers may have influenced the Houma's departure from their ancestral village; by 1709, they had fled south to Bayou LaFourche. After the 1763 Treaty of Paris, which transferred French lands west of the Mississippi to Spain and those east of the river to England, the Houma found themselves under the authority of two colonial powers. Their hunting grounds were now under English rule, while their villages lay within Spanish boundaries. The Houma came under American rule following the Louisiana Purchase of 1803, although land grants from the French and Spanish were not honored.

6. Mike Tidwell, *Bayou Farewell: The Rich Life and Tragic Death of Louisiana's Cajun Coast* (NY: Vintage Books, 2004), 7.

7. Van Heerden and Bryan, *The Storm*, 163–65. For an interesting discussion on early views of wetlands, see Prince, *Wetlands of the American Midwest*.

8. Filmmaker Spike Lee riffs on the title of this song in his documentary on Hurricane Katrina, *When the Levees Broke: A Requiem in Four Acts* (New York: 40 Acres and a Mule Filmworks, 2006), DVD.

9. Robert N. Jenkins, "From New Orleans' Founding, Riches Outweighed Risks," *St. Petersburg Times*, September 4, 2005. http://www.sptimes.com/2005/09/04/Worldandnation/From_New_Orleans__fou.shtml.

10. Ken Wells, "Collapsing Marsh Dwarfs BP Oil Blowout as Ecological Disaster," *Bloomberg News*, August 17, 2010. http://www.bloomberg.com/news/2010-08-18/

collapsing-louisiana-marsh-dwarfs-bp-oil-blowout-as-environmental-disaster.
html.

11. Brown Marsh Data Information Management System, "Brown Marsh Q & A."
http://brownmarsh.com/qa.htm#What%20is%20the%20Brown%20
Marsh%20phenomenon.

12. Van Heerden, *The Storm*, 169.

13. Robert Twilley, interview in *WaterMarks: Louisiana Coastal Wetlands Planning,
Protection and Restoration News*, February 22, 2003, 19.

14. Thomas Mayheart Dardar Jr., "Testimony of Chief Thomas Dardar, Jr.,
Principal Chief of the United Houma Nation Before the Senate Committee
on Indian Affairs," U.S. Senate, July 19, 2012.

15. Coastal Wetlands Planning, Protection and Restoration Act, Managing
Agencies, "Wetland Loss in Louisiana," 1997. https://lacoast.gov/reports/
rtc/1997/5.htm.

16. Personal interview with Michael T. Mayheart Dardar, September 26, 2012.

17. "Homeland in Peril: United Houma Nation Tribe Member Leah Dardar
Savoy." YouTube video, 9:01. Posted February 4, 2010, by healthygulf1. http://
www.youtube.com/watch?v=6SDItWGI9YY.

18. The Kresge Foundation, "Nonprofits Work with Gulf Coast Communities to
Respond to Climate Change," September 6, 2011. http://www.kresge.org/
news/nonprofits-work-gulf-coast-communities-respond-climate-change.

19. David Holthouse and Priscilla Holthouse, "The Houma Nation Digs Out,"
The American Prospect 20.2 (2009): A17–A18.

20. Ibid.

21. Ibid.

22. Quoted in Rocky Kistner, "A Gulf Chorus Fights BP's PR War," *The Energy
Collective*, December 31, 2011. http://theenergycollective.com/rockykistner/
73386/gulf-chorus-fights-bps-pr-war.

23. Gina M. Solomon and Sarah Janssen, "Health Effects of the Gulf Oil Spill,"
The Journal of the American Medical Association 304.10 (2010): 1118–19.

24. Lizzy Ratner, "A Brief Story of Dispossession, American-Style—and What You
Can Do About It," *Mondoweiss: The War of Ideas in the Middle East*, November 30,
2011. http://mondoweiss.net/2011/11/a-brief-story-of-dispossession-american
style-%E2%80%93-and-what-you-can-do-about-it.html.

25. See Michel Martin, "Native American Group Hit Hard by Oil Spill," National
Public Radio, June 3, 2010. http://www.npr.org/templates/story/story.
php?storyId=127405886.

26. Testimony of Brenda Dardar Robichaux, "House Committee on Natural

Resources Oversight Hearing Gulf of Mexico: A Focus on Community Recovery and New Response Technology," April 18, 2011.

27. Ibid.

28. Louisiana Coastal Wetlands Conservation and Restoration Task Force and the Wetlands Conservation and Restoration Authority, *Coast 2050: Toward a Sustainable Coastal Louisiana* (Baton Rouge: Louisiana Department of Natural Resources, 1998), 7.

29. Thomas Mayheart Dardar Jr., "Testimony of Chief Thomas Dardar, Jr., Principal Chief of the United Houma Nation Before the Senate Committee on Indian Affairs," U.S. Senate, July 19, 2012.

30. Frank McMains, "The United Houma Nation, Staying Afloat," *Indian Country Today Media Network*, October 6, 2011. http://indiancountrytoday medianetwork.com/2011/10/06/united-houma-nation-staying-afloat-57153.

31. "United Houma Nation Youth Media Lab." YouTube video, 2:15. Posted August 13, 2010, by Bridge the Gulf Project. http://www.youtube.com/watch?v=wYT6-Bftmig.

32. Ibid.

33. Ibid.

34. "Lora Ann Chaisson, United Houma Nation Tribal Member." YouTube video, 3:25. Posted August 26, 2010, by Bridge the Gulf Project. http://www.youtube.com/watch?v=FXWUhIle-L4.

35. "Unheard Voices from the Gulf Coast: United Houma Nation." YouTube video, 3:23. Posted June 25, 2010, by greenforall. http://www.youtube.com/watch?v=of3qEhDbi1Y.

36. Dizzydean, "The Chitimacha [*sic*] Face Another Storm," *The Daily Kos*, August 31, 2008. http://www.dailykos.com/story/2008/08/31/581302/-The-Chitimacha-Face-Another-Storm#.

37. Loretta J. Ross, "A Feminist Perspective on Katrina," in *The Women of Katrina*, 20–21.

38. United States Environmental Protection Agency, "Alaska Impacts and Adaptation." http://www.epa.gov/climatechange/impacts-adaptation/alaska.html#ImpactsAlaska. "Infrastructure damage" is an all-encompassing term comprising damaged paved roads, highways, sewage and water systems, and buildings. Thawing permafrost results in the buckling of roads, the breakage of pipes, and the subsidence of land.

39. NANA Regional Corporation, Inc., "Kivalina Village Profile." http://nana.com/files/pdf-bios/NANA-VillageProfile-Kivalina.pdf. The NANA Regional Corporation is a regional Alaska Native corporation formed under the Alaska Native Land Claims Settlement Act.

40. Ibid.

41. City of Kivalina, Alaska, Local Hazards Mitigation Plan. Approved by the Kivalina City Council on November 9, 2007, and by FEMA on December 14, 2007. http://www.commerce.state.ak.us/dca/planning/nfip/Hazard_ Mitigation_Plans/Kivalina_HMP.pdf.

42. Christine Shearer, *Kivalina: A Climate Change Story* (Chicago, IL: Haymarket Books, 2011), 15.

43. Ibid., 15. See also Rebecca Tsosie, "Indigenous People and Environmental Justice: The Impact of Climate Change," *University of Colorado Law Review* 78 (2007): 1625–39.

44. Robert J. Martin, "The Village of Kivalina Is Falling into the Sea: Should CERCLA Section 9626(b) Be Available to Move the Village from Harm's Way?" *Environmental and Earth Law Journal (EELJ)* 2.1 (2006): 1–32.

45. Shearer, *Kivalina*, 15.

46. "Kivalina, AK Storm, 11/9/2011." YouTube video, 1:00. Posted November 11, 2011, by midaswanify. http://www.youtube.com/watch?v=DEk4gqo50Ec.

47. Quoted in Shearer, *Kivalina*, 139.

48. Alan Zarembo, "An Alaskan Island Finds Itself Losing Ground," *Los Angeles Times*, November 25, 2007. http://articles.latimes.com/2007/nov/25/science/ sci-kivalina25.

49. Martin, "The Village of Kivalina," 6–7.

50. Ibid., 142.

51. Ibid., 8.

52. Quoted in Shearer, *Kivalina*, 147.

53. Daniel Cordalis and Dean B. Suagee, "The Effects of Climate Change on American Indian and Alaska Native Tribes," *Natural Resources & Environment* 22 (2007–2008): 45.

54. Quoted in Shearer, *Kivalina*, 147.

55. Shearer, *Kivalina*, 7.

56. Cordalis and Suagee, "The Effects of Climate Change ," 45.

57. Dana Lixenberg, *The Last Days of Shishmaref* (Edam and Rotterdam, Netherlands: Paradox/Episode Publishing, 2008), 5.

58. Ibid., 83.

59. Luci Eningowuk, "Testimony of the Shishmaref Erosion and Relocation Coalition Before the Committee on Appropriations of the United States Senate, June 20, 2004," Hearing on Alaska Native Villages Affected by Flooding and Erosion, U.S. Government Printing Office. http://www.gpo.

gov/fdsys/browse/collection.action?collectionCode=CHRG&browsePath=108%2FSENATE%2FCommittee+on+Appropriations&isCollapsed=false&leafLevelBrowse=false&isDocumentResults=true&ycord=126.

60. Caleb Pungowiyi, "Native Observations of Change in the Marine Environment of the Bering Strait Region," *National Oceanic and Atmospheric Administration Arctic Theme Page.* http://www.arctic.noaa.gov/essay_pungowiyi.html.

61. See Pungowiyi, "Native Observations" for a detailed account of the changes in the Arctic environment.

62. Eningowuk, "Testimony," 2.

63. Rachel M. Gregg, "Relocating the Native Village of Shishmaref, Alaska Due to Coastal Erosion," *Climate Adaptation Knowledge Exchange*, December 18, 2010.http://www.cakex.org/case-studies/relocating-native-village-shishmaref-alaska-due-coastal-erosion.

64. Eningowuk, "Testimony," 2–3.

65. The ten to fifteen years began in 2004, when the Army Corps made its assessment of relocation costs.

66. Quoted in Nancy Lord, *Early Warming: Crisis and Response in the Climate-Changed North* (Berkeley, CA: Counterpoint, 2012), 142.

67. Eningowuk, "Testimony," 6.

68. Clarence Alexander, Nora Bynum, Elizabeth Johnson, et al., "Linking Indigenous and Scientific Knowledge of Climate Change," *Bioscience* 61.6 (2011): 477.

CONCLUSION

1. Idle No More cofounder Jessica Gordon sent out the first tweet with the hashtag #IdleNoMore on October 30, 2012. It read: "awesome day of laying the groundwork for rally and petitions opposing #omnibus #billc45 re #indianact please find our fb group #IDLE NO MORE." Idle No More, "Living History." http://www.idlenomore.ca/living-history.

2. "Idle No More—Steve Rushton Interviews Sylvia McAdam," radio interview, 23:17. January 28, 2013. *Occupy Radio LDN.* http://www.mixcloud.com/markweaver5015/idle-no-more-steve-rushton-interviews-sylvia-mcadam.

3. Lorraine Land, Liora Zimmerman, and Andrea Bradley, "A Summary of Current Federal Legislative Amendments Affecting First Nations," Olthius Kleer Townshend LLP (December 20, 2012). http://www.anglican.ca/im/files/2013/01/legamend.pdf.

4. "CTV News Channel, Tantoo Cardinal on Idle No More, January 16, 2013." YouTube video, 8:42. Posted January 17, 2013, by MsBeautifulRed. http://www.youtube.com/watch?feature=endscreen&NR=1&v=Paxc3bA7qvY.

5. "Idle No More Alberta—Dr. Pam Palmater (Part 1 of 4)." YouTube video, 14:01. Posted December 3, 2012, by Karri-Lynn Paul. http://www.youtube.com/watch?v=STatNSjcrvo.

6. Ibid.

7. Lisa Charleyboy, "Idle No More: Canada's Indigenous People Are Demanding a Better Deal," *Guardian*, January 11, 2013. http://www.theguardian.com/commentisfree/2013/jan/11/canada-indigenous-people-demand-better-deal.

8. Jordan Press and Michael Woods, "Idle No More Movement 'Different' from Anything the Government Had Ever Seen Before, Documents Reveal," *Vancouver Sun*, April 10, 2013.

9. Ibid.

10. Ibid.

11. A round dance is traditional to many indigenous nations; as its name suggests, it takes the form of a circle. For an example of the first flash mob round dance at Cornwall Centre in Regina, Saskatchewan, please refer to the YouTube video "Idlenomore—Regina Round Dance Flash Mob." 8:12. Posted December 17, 2012, by Smokey01Smoke. http://www.youtube.com/watch?v=QA_Hn84SrCM.

12. Sheila Regan, "Idle No More Flash Roundy Fills Mall of America Rotunda," *Twin Cities Daily Planet*, December 29, 2012. http://www.tcdailyplanet.net/news/2012/12/30/idle-no-more-flash-roundy-mall-america.

13. Ibid.

14. Rebekka Schlichting, "Native Americans, Supporters Put on Flash Mob Demonstration in South Park for Idle No More," *Lawrence Journal-World*, January 12, 2013. http://www2.ljworld.com/news/2013/jan/12/hundreds-native-americans-flash-mob-south-park-idl/.

15. *The National*, CBC News, "Countdown to Friday: Explaining Idle No More." YouTube video, 18:14. Posted January 8, 2013, by The National. http://www.youtube.com/watch?v=sSdY_FVsGgo.

16. Ibid.

17. Ibid.

18. Ibid.

19. Wab Kinew, "Idle No More Is Not Just an 'Indian Thing,'" *Huffington Post Canada*, December 17, 2012. http://www.huffingtonpost.ca/wab-kinew/idle-no-more-canada_b_2316098.html.

20. Quoted in Kinew," Idle No More."

21. See the Idle No More website, http://www.idlenomore.ca, and the "Sovereignty Summer Begins" Facebook page, https://www.facebook.com/events/605413289491688/.

22. "Sovereignty Summer Begins" Facebook page. https://www.facebook.com/events/605413289491688/.

23. "Idle No More—Calls for Change." http://www.idlenomore.ca/calls_for_change.

24. This incident received media coverage in the United States, but not in Canada. See Rick Rojas, "Tribal Activists Block Shipment through Idaho Wilderness," *Los Angeles Times*, August 7, 2013, http://articles.latimes.com/2013/aug/07/nation/la-na-0808-tar-sands-20130808; "Idaho Tribe Files Suit to Halt Megaload Headed to Tar Sands," *Los Angeles Times*, August 9, 2013, http://articles.latimes.com/2013/aug/09/nation/la-na-nn-nez-perce-megaload-lawsuit-20130809; and "Judge Rules against 'Megaloads' of Tar Sands Equipment in Idaho," *Los Angeles Times*, September 13, 2013, http://www.latimes.com/nation/la-na-mega-load-20130914-story.html.

25. Martin Lukacs, "New Brunswick Fracking Protests Are the Frontline of a Democratic Fight," *Guardian*, October 21, 2013. http://www.theguardian.com/environment/2013/oct/21/new-brunswick-fracking-protests.

26. Ibid.

27. Dylan Powell, "The 24 Hour Elsipogtog Raid Timeline," October 23, 2013. http://dylanxpowell.com/2013/10/23/the-24-hour-elsipogtog-raid-timeline/.

28. "Elsipogtog: RCMP Move in on Peaceful Protesters 17 October." YouTube video, 2:21. Posted October 17, 2013 by Chris Sabas. http://www.youtube.com/watch?v=MAWPSv2Vfkw.

29. Lukacs, "New Brunswick Fracking Protests."

30. "Idle No More—Steve Rushton Interviews Sylvia McAdam."

31. "CTV News Channel, Tantoo Cardinal on Idle No More, January 16, 2013."

BIBLIOGRAPHY

Abate, Randall S. and Elizabeth Ann Kronk. *Climate Change and Indigenous Peoples: The Search for Legal Remedies.* Northampton, MA: Edward Elgar Publishing, 2013.

Adamson, Joni. *American Indian Literature, Environmental Justice, and Ecocriticism: The Middle Place.* Tucson: University of Arizona Press, 2001.

———, Mei Mei Evans, and Rachel Stein, eds. *The Environmental Justice Reader: Politics, Poetics, and Pedagogy.* Tucson: University of Arizona Press, 2002.

———, and Scott Slovic. "The Shoulders We Stand On: An Introduction to Ethnicity and Ecocriticism." *MELUS: Multi-Ethnic Literature of the United States* 34.2 (2009): 5–24.

Albers, Patricia and Beatrice Medicine, eds. *The Hidden Half: Studies of Plains Indian Women.* Boston, MA: University Press of America, 1983.

Alberts, Crystal. "In the Talking Leaves: Diane Glancy's Reclamation of Voice and Archive." In *The Salt Companion to Diane Glancy*, edited by James Mackay, 114–34. London: Salt Publishing, 2010.

Alexander, Clarence, Nora Bynum, Elizabeth Johnson, et al. "Linking Indigenous and Scientific Knowledge of Climate Change." *Bioscience* 61.6 (2011): 477–84.

Alfred, Taiaiake. *Wasáse: Indigenous Pathways of Action and Freedom.* Peterborough, ON: Broadview Press, 2005.

Allen, Chadwick. "Postcolonial Theory and the Discourse of Treaties." *American Quarterly* 52.1 (2001): 59–89.

———. *Trans-Indigenous: Methodologies for Global Native Literary Studies.* Minneapolis: University of Minnesota Press, 2012.

Allen, Paula Gunn. *The Sacred Hoop: Recovering the Feminine in American Indian Traditions.* Boston, MA: Beacon Press, 1984.

Andrews, Jennifer. "A Conversation with Diane Glancy." *American Indian Quarterly* 26.4 (2002): 645–58.

Armstrong, Jeannette. "Kwtlakin? What Is Your Place?" In *What Is Your Place? Indigeneity and Immigration in Canada*, edited by Hartmut Lutz, 29–33. Augsburg, Germany: Wissner-Verlag, 2007.

Aun-nish-e-naubay (Patrick Gourneau). *History of the Turtle Mountain Band of*

Chippewa Indians. N.p., n.d. Special Collections of the Chester Fritz Library of the University of North Dakota.

Awiakta, Marylou. *Abiding Appalachia: Where Mountain and Atom Meet.* Memphis, TN: St. Martin's Press, 1978.

————. "Red Clay." In *Aniyunwiya/Real Human Beings: An Anthology of Contemporary Cherokee Prose,* edited by Joseph Bruchac, 29–41. Greenfield Center, NY: Greenfield Review Press, 1995.

Baker University Wetlands. http://www.bakeru.edu/wetlands/species-lists.

Barnouw, Victor. *Wisconsin Chippewa Myths and Tales.* Madison: University of Wisconsin Press, 1977.

Basso, Keith H. *Wisdom Sits in Places: Landscape and Language Among the Western Apache.* Albuquerque: University of New Mexico Press, 1996.

Baxter, R. M. "Environmental Effects of Dams and Impoundments." *Annual Review of Ecology and Systematics* 8 (1977): 255–83.

Belin, Esther G. "Directional Beauty." In *From the Belly of My Beauty.* Tucson: University of Arizona Press, 1999.

Benton-Banai, Edward. *The Mishomis Book: The Voice of the Ojibway.* Hayward, WI: Indian Country Communications, 1988.

Bernd, Candice. "Idle No More: From Grassroots to Global Movement." *Truthout* 29 (January 2013). http://truth-out.org/news/item/14165-idle-no-more-from-grassroots-to—global-movement.

Blaeser, Kimberly M. "Like 'Reeds through the Ribs of a Basket': Native Women Weaving Stories." *American Indian Quarterly* 21.4 (1997): 555–65.

Boelhower, William Q. *Through a Glass Darkly: Ethnic Semiosis in American Literature.* New York: Oxford University Press, 1987.

Bosque Redondo Memorial. "Welcome to the Bosque Redondo Memorial." http://www.bosqueredondomemorial.com/.

Bowman, Greg, and Janel Curry-Roper. *The Houma People of Louisiana: A Story of Indian Survival.* Houma, LA: The United Houma Nation, 1982.

Brasseaux, Carl A. *French, Cajun, Creole, Houma: A Primer on Francophone Louisiana.* Baton Rouge: Louisiana State University Press, 2005.

Brehm, Victoria. "The Metamorphoses of an Ojibwa *Manido*." *American Literature* 68.4 (1996): 677–706.

Brooks, Lisa. *The Common Pot: The Recovery of Native Space in the Northeast.* Minneapolis: University of Minnesota Press, 2008.

Brown, Alleen. "This Land Is Our Land: How a 19th-Century Law Led to the Federal Government's Largest Payout Ever." *In These Times* 35.7 (2011): 14–21.

Brown Marsh Data Information Management System. "Brown Marsh Q & A." http://brownmarsh.com/qa.htm#What%20is%20the%20Brown%20 Marsh%20phenomenon.

Bruchac, Joseph. *Survival This Way: Interviews with American Indian Poets.* Tucson: University of Arizona Press, 1987.

Buffalohead, Priscilla K. "Farmers, Warriors, Traders: A Fresh Look at Ojibway Women." *Minnesota History* 48.6 (1983): 236–44.

Burley, David M. *Losing Ground: Identity and Land Loss in Coastal Louisiana.* Jackson: University of Mississippi Press, 2010.

Burns, Carol, dir. *Mni Sose (aka Missouri River).* Kansas City, KS: 2010. DVD.

Byrd, Jodi A. *The Transit of Empire: Indigenous Critiques of Colonialism.* Minneapolis: University of Minnesota Press, 2011.

Cajete, Gregory. *Native Science.* Santa Fe, NM: Clear Light Books, 2000.

Camp, Gregory S. "Working Out Their Own Salvation: The Allotment of Land in Severalty and the Turtle Mountain Chippewa Band, 1870–1920." *American Indian Culture and Research Journal* 14 (1990): 19–38.

Castor, Laura Virginia. "Claiming Place in Wor(l)ds: Linda Hogan's *Solar Storms.*" *MELUS: Multi-Ethnic Literature of the United States* 31.2 (2006): 157–80.

CBC News. "9 Questions about Idle No More," January 5, 2013. http://www.cbc. ca/news/canada/9-questions-about-idle-no-more-1.1301843.

Charles-Newton, Eugenia, and Elizabeth Ann Kronk. "Introduction to Indigenous Sovereignty Under International and Domestic Law." In *Climate Change and Indigenous Peoples: The Search for Legal Remedies,* edited by Randall S. Abate and Elizabeth Ann Kronk. Northampton, MA: Edward Elgar Publishing, 2013.

Charleyboy, Lisa. "Idle No More: Canada's Indigenous People Are Demanding a Better Deal." *The Guardian,* January 11, 2013. http://www.theguardian.com/ commentisfree/2013/jan/11/canada-indigenous-people-demand-better-deal.

Cherokee Heritage Center. http://www.cherokeeheritage.org/.

Cherokee Nation. *The Constitution and Laws of the Cherokee Nation: Passed at Tah-Le-Quah, Cherokee Nation, 1839.* Wilmington, DE: Scholars Resource, Inc., 1975.

Cheyfitz, Eric. "The (Post)Colonial Construction of Indian Country: U.S. American Indian Literatures and Federal Indian Law." In *The Columbia Guide to American Indian Literatures of the United States Since 1945,* edited by Eric Cheyfitz, 1–126. New York: Columbia University Press, 2004.

Child, Brenda J. *Holding Our World Together: Ojibwe Women and the Survival of Community.* New York: Viking Press, 2012.

Clark, Sharri. "Representing Native Identity: The Trail of Tears and the Cherokee Heritage Center in Oklahoma." *Cultural Survival Quarterly* 21.1 (1997): 36–40.

Coastal Wetlands Planning, Protection and Restoration Act, Managing Agencies. "Wetland Loss in Louisiana." 1997. http://www.lacoast.gov/reports/rtc/1997/5.htm.

Cohen, Felix S. *Handbook of Federal Indian Law.* Albuquerque: University of New Mexico Press, 1971.

Conley, Robert J. *The Dark Way.* Norman: University of Oklahoma Press, 2000.

———. *The Peace Chief: A Novel of the Real People.* New York: St. Martin's Press, 1998.

———. *Sequoyah: A Novel of the Real People.* Norman: University of Oklahoma Press, 2002.

———. *The Way of the Priests.* Norman: University of Oklahoma Press, 2000.

———. *The White Path.* Norman: University of Oklahoma Press, 2000.

Cook, Barbara J., ed. *From the Center of Tradition: Critical Perspectives on Linda Hogan.* Boulder: University of Colorado Press, 2003.

Cook-Lynn, Elizabeth. *Aurelia: A Crow Creek Trilogy.* Niwot: University of Colorado Press, 1999.

———. *From the River's Edge.* New York: Arcade Publishing, 1991.

———. "A Mixed-Blood, Tribeless Voice in American Indian Literatures: Michael Dorris." In *Anti-Indianism in Modern America: A Voice from Tatekeya's Earth,* 72–90. Urbana: University of Illinois Press, 2001.

———. *Then Badger Said This.* Fairfield, WA: Ye Galleon Press, 1983.

———. *Why I Can't Read Wallace Stegner and Other Essays: A Tribal Voice.* Madison: University of Wisconsin Press, 1996.

Cordalis, Daniel, and Dean B. Suagee. "The Effects of Climate Change on American Indian and Alaska Native Tribes." *Natural Resources & Environment* 22 (2007–2008): 45.

Coulthard, Glen Sean. *Red Masks, White Skin: Rejecting the Colonial Politics of Recognition.* Minneapolis: University of Minnesota Press, 2014.

Couser, G. Thomas. "Tracing the Trickster: Nanapush, Ojibwe Oral Tradition, and *Tracks.*" In *Approaches to Teaching the Works of Louise Erdrich,* edited by Greg Sarris, Connie A. Jacobs, and James R. Giles. New York: The Modern Language Association of America, 2004.

"The Crying Indian—full commercial—Keep America Beautiful." April 22 (Earth Day), 1971. YouTube video, 1:00. Posted by coffeekid99. https://www.youtube.com/watch?v=j7OHG7tHrNM.

"CTV News Channel, Tantoo Cardinal on Idle No More, January 16, 2013."
YouTube video, 8:42. Posted January 17, 2013, by MsBeautifulRed. http://
www.youtube.com/watch?feature=endscreen&NR=1&v=Paxc3bA7qvY.

Dankelman, Irene, ed. *Gender and Climate Change: An Introduction*. London:
Earthscan, Ltd., 2010.

Danker, Kathleen. "'The Violation of the Earth': Elizabeth Cook-Lynn's *From the
River's Edge* in the Historical Context of the Pick-Sloan Missouri River Dam
Project." *Wicazo Sa Review* 12.2 (1997): 85–93.

Dardar, Thomas, Jr. "Tales of Wind and Water: Houma Indians and Hurricanes."
American Indian Culture and Research Journal 32.2 (2008): 27–32.

———. "Testimony of Chief Thomas Dardar, Jr., Principal Chief of the United
Houma Nation Before the Senate Committee on Indian Affairs." U.S.
Senate, July 19, 2012.

David, Emmanuel, and Elaine Enarson. *The Women of Katrina: How Gender, Race,
and Class Matter in an American Disaster*. Nashville, TN: Vanderbilt
University Press, 2012.

DePriest, Maria. "Once Upon a Time, Today: Hearing Fleur's Voice in *Tracks*."
Journal of Narrative Theory 38.2 (2008): 249–68.

Dizzydean. "The Chitimacha [*sic*] Face Another Storm." *The Daily Kos*, August 31,
2008. http://www.dailykos.com/story/2008/08/31/581302/-The-Chitimacha-Face-
Another-Storm#.

Duncan, Barbara, ed. *Living Stories of the Cherokee*. Chapel Hill: University of
North Carolina Press, 1998.

Duthu, N. Bruce. *American Indians and the Law*. New York: Penguin Books, 2008.

Elias, Amy. "Fragments That Rune Up the Shores: *Pushing the Bear*, Coyote
Aesthetics, and Recovered History." *Modern Fiction Studies* 45.1 (1999): 185–211.

Ellinghaus, Katherine. "The Benefits of Being Indian: Blood Quanta,
Intermarriage, and Allotment Policy on the White Earth Reservation,
1889–1920." *Frontiers: A Journal of Women Studies* 29.2–3 (2008): 81–105.

"Elsipogtog: RCMP Move in on Peaceful Protesters 17 October." YouTube video,
2:21. Posted October 17, 2013, by Chris Sabas. http://www.youtube.com/
watch?v=MAWPSv2Vfkw.

Eningowuk, Luci. "Testimony of the Shishmaref Erosion and Relocation Coalition
Before the Committee on Appropriations of the United States Senate, June 20,
2004." Hearing on Alaska Native Villages Affected by Flooding and Erosion.
U.S. Government Printing Office. http://www.gpo.gov/fdsys/browse/collection
.action?collectionCode=CHRG&browsePath=108%2FSENATE%2FCommittee
+on+Appropriations&isCollapsed=false&leafLevelBrowse=false&isDocument
Results=true&ycord=126.

Erdrich, Lise. "Corn Is Number One." In *Night Train*, 26–31. Minneapolis, MN: Coffee House Press, 2008.

Erdrich, Louise. *The Bingo Palace*. New York: HarperCollins Publishers, 1994.

———. *Books and Islands in Ojibwe Country*. Washington, D.C.: National Geographic Society, 2003.

———. *Four Souls*. New York: HarperCollins Publishers, 2004.

———. *The Last Report on the Miracles at Little No Horse*. New York: HarperCollins Publishers, 2001.

———. *Love Medicine*. Expanded ed. New York: HarperCollins Publishers, 2000.

———. *The Plague of Doves*. New York: HarperCollins Publishers, 2008.

———. "Rape on the Reservation." *New York Times*, February 26, 2013. http://www.nytimes.com/2013/02/27/opinion/native-americans-and-the-violence-against-women-act.html.

———. *The Round House*. New York: HarperCollins Publishers, 2012.

———. "A Time for Human Rights on Native Ground." *New York Times*, December 29, 2000. http://www.nytimes.com/2000/12/29/opinion/29ERDR.html.

———. *Tracks*. New York: Harper & Row, 1988.

———, and Michael Dorris. "Who Owns the Land?" *New York Times Magazine*, September 4, 1988. http://www.nytimes.com/1988/10/02/magazine/l-who-owns-the-land-322388.html.

Fitz, Karsten. "Employing the Strategy of Transculturation: Colonial Migration and Postcolonial Interpretation in Diane Glancy's *Pushing the Bear*." *Zietschrift für Anglistik und Amerikanistik: A Quarterly of Language, Literature and Culture* 49.3 (2001): 243–32.

———. "Native and Christian: Religion and Spirituality as Transcultural Negotiation in American Indian Novels of the 1990s." *American Indian Culture and Research Journal* 26.2 (2002): 1–15.

Foreman, Grant. *Indian Removal: The Emigration of the Five Civilized Tribes of Indians*. Norman: University of Oklahoma Press, 1953.

Friedman, Susan Stanford. "Identity Politics, Syncretism, Catholicism, and Anishinabe Religion in Louise Erdrich's *Tracks*." *Religion and Literature* 26 (1994): 107–33.

Gedicks, Al. *The New Resource Wars: Native and Environmental Struggles Against Multinational Corporations*. Boston, MA: South End Press, 1993.

The General Allotment Act of 1887. 25 U.S.C. 331 (1887).

Glancy, Diane. *Pushing the Bear: After the Trail of Tears*. Norman: University of Oklahoma Press, 2009.

————. *Pushing the Bear: A Novel of the Trail of Tears.* San Diego, CA: Harcourt Brace, 1996.

"Grandma Margaret's Long Walk Story." YouTube video, 7:48. Posted March 3, 2009, by daybreakwarrior. https://www.youtube.com/watch?v=d85Q1U_f-l4.

Gregg, Rachel M. "Relocating the Native Village of Shishmaref, Alaska Due to Coastal Erosion." *Climate Adaptation Knowledge Exchange,* December 18, 2010. http://www.cakex.org/case-studies/relocating-native-village-shishmaref-alaska-due-coastal-erosion.

Grijalva, James M. *Closing the Circle: Environmental Justice in Indian Country.* Durham, NC: Carolina Academic Press, 2008.

Gross, Lawrence. "The Trickster and World Maintenance: An Anishinaabe Reading of Louise Erdrich's *Tracks.*" *Studies in American Indian Literatures* 17.3 (Fall 2005): 48–66.

Hada, Kenneth. "Even the Snow Is White: Displacement and Literary Ecology in Diane Glancy's *Pushing the Bear.*" *American Indian Culture and Research Journal* 33:1 (2009): 131–42.

Hale, Frederick. "Axiological Dissonance and Moral Accountability in Elizabeth Cook-Lynn's *From the River's Edge.*" *European Review of Native American Studies* 14.1 (2000): 39–44.

Harcourt, Wendy, and Arturo Escobar. *Women and the Politics of Place.* Bloomfield, CT: Kumarian Press, 2005.

Hausman, Blake. *Riding the Trail of Tears.* Lincoln, NE: Bison Books, 2011.

Heise, Ursula K. *Sense of Place and Sense of Planet: The Environmental Imagination of the Global.* New York: Oxford University Press, 2008.

Hogan, Linda. *Dwellings: A Spiritual History of the Living World.* New York: Scribner, 1995.

————. "An Interview with Linda Hogan." *The Missouri Review* 17 (1994): 109–34.

————. *Solar Storms.* New York: Simon & Schuster, 1995.

Holthouse, David, and Priscilla Holthouse. "The Houma Nation Digs Out." *The American Prospect* 20.2 (2009): A17–A18.

"Homeland in Peril: United Houma Nation Tribe Member Leah Dardar Savoy." YouTube video, 9:01. Posted February 4, 2010, by healthygulfi. http://www.youtube.com/watch?v=6SDItWGI9YY.

Hopley, Scott, and Susan Ross. "Aboriginal Claims to Water Rights Grounded in the Principle Ad Medium Filum Aquae, Riparian Rights and the Winters Doctrine." *Journal of Environmental Law & Practice* 19 (2009): 225.

Howe, Craig, and Kim Tall Bear, eds. *This Stretch of the River: Lakota, Dakota, and*

Nakota Responses to the Lewis and Clark Expedition and Bicentennial. Sioux Falls, SD: Oak Lake Writers' Society & Pine Hill Press, 2006.

Huhndorf, Shari M. *Mapping the Americas: The Transnational Politics of Contemporary Native Culture.* Ithaca, NY: Cornell University Press, 2009.

Huus, Kari. "Houma Indians and the Gulf Oil Spill." Manataka American Indian Council. N.d. http://www.manataka.org/page2187.html.

Idle No More. "Idle No More Calls for Mass Action on October 7th!" http://www.idlenomore.ca/idle_no_more_calls_for_mass_action_on_Oct_7th.

"Idle No More Alberta—Dr. Pam Palmater (Part 1 of 4)." YouTube video, 14:01. Posted December 3, 2012, by Karri-Lynn Paul. http://www.youtube.com/watch?v=STatNSjcrvo.

"Idlenomore—Regina Round Dance Flash Mob." YouTube video, 8:12. Posted December 17, 2012, by Smokey01Smoke. http://www.youtube.com/watch?v=QA_Hn84SrCM.

Jacobs, Sue-Ellen, Wesley Thomas, and Sabine Lang, eds. *Two Spirit People: Native American Gender Identity, Sexuality, and Spirituality.* Urbana and London: University of Illinois Press, 1997.

Jenkins, Robert N. "From New Orleans' Founding, Riches Outweighed Risks." *St. Petersburg Times*, September 4, 2005. http://www.sptimes.com/2005/09/04/Worldandnation/From_New_Orleans_fou.shtml.

Jespersen, T. Christine. "Unmapping Adventure: Sewing Resistance in Linda Hogan's *Solar Storms*." *Western American Literature* 45.3 (2010): 274–300.

Johnson, Brad. "Western Voices Interview with Linda Hogan." Center of the American West, March 2, 1998. http://www.centerwest.org/voices/Hogan-interview.htm.

Johnson, Kelli Lyon. "Writing Deeper Maps: Mapmaking, Local Indigenous Knowledges, and Literary Nationalism in Native Women's Writing." *Studies in American Indian Literatures* 19.4 (2007): 103–20.

Johnston, Basil. *The Manitous: The Spiritual World of the Ojibways.* New York: HarperCollins Publishers, 1995.

———. *Ojibway Heritage.* Lincoln and London: University of Nebraska Press, 1990.

Johnston, Carolyn Ross. *Cherokee Women in Crisis: Trail of Tears, Civil War, and Allotment, 1838–1907.* Tuscaloosa: University of Alabama Press, 2003.

Juhasz, Antonia. *Black Tide: The Devastating Impact of the Gulf Oil Spill.* New York: John Wiley and Sons, 2011.

Justice, Daniel Heath. *Our Fire Survives the Storm: A Cherokee Literary History.* Minneapolis: University of Minnesota Press, 2006.

Kearney, Michael S., J. C. Alexis Riter, and R. Eugene Turner. "Freshwater River Diversions for Marsh Restoration in Louisiana: Twenty-Six Years of Changing Vegetative Cover and Marsh Area." *Geophysical Research Letters* 38.16, L16405 (2011).

Keys, Lucy Hoyt Lowrey. "Historical Sketches of the Cherokees, Together with Some of Their Customs, Traditions, and Superstitions." In *Native American Women's Writing, 1800–1924*, edited by Karen Kilcup, 71–89. New York: Wiley-Blackwell, 2000.

Kilpatrick, Jack Frederick, and Anna Gritts Kilpatrick. *New Echota Letters*. Dallas, TX: Southern Methodist University Press, 1968.

Kinew, Wab. "Idle No More Is Not Just an 'Indian Thing.'" *Huffington Post Canada*, December 17, 2012. http://www.huffingtonpost.ca/wab-kinew/idle -no-more-canada_b_2316098.html.

Kistner, Rocky. "A Gulf Chorus Fights BP's PR War." *The Energy Collective*, December 31, 2011. http://theenergycollective.com/rockykistner/73386/ gulf-chorus-fights-bps-pr-war.

"Kivalina, AK Storm, 11/9/2011." YouTube video, 1:00. Posted November 11, 2011, by midaswanify. http://www.youtube.com/watch?v=DEk4gq050Ec.

Konkle, Maureen. *Writing Indian Nations: Native Intellectuals and the Politics of Historiography, 1827–1863*. Chapel Hill: University of North Carolina Press, 2004.

Kovach, Margaret. *Indigenous Methodologies: Characteristics, Conversations, and Contexts*. Toronto: University of Toronto Press, 2009.

Krech, Shephard. *The Ecological Indian: Myth and History*. New York: W. W. Norton, 1999.

Kresge Foundation, The. "Nonprofits Work with Gulf Coast Communities to Respond to Climate Change." September 6, 2011. http://www.kresge.org/ news/nonprofits-work-gulf-coast-communities-respond-climate-change.

Krupat, Arnold. "Representing Cherokee Dispossession." *Studies in American Indian Literatures* 17.1 (2005): 16–41.

Land, Lorraine, Liora Zimmerman, and Andrea Bradley. "A Summary of Current Federal Legislative Amendments Affecting First Nations." Olthius Kleer Townshend LLP (December 20, 2012). http://www.anglican.ca/im/files/ 2013/01/legamend.pdf.

Lawrence, Adrea, and Brec Cooke. "Law, Language, and Land: A Multimethod Analysis of the General Allotment Act and Its Discourses." *Qualitative Inquiry* 16.3 (2010): 217–29.

Lawson, Michael L. *Dammed Indians: The Pick-Sloan Plan and the Missouri River Sioux, 1944–1980*. Norman: University of Oklahoma Press, 1982.

Lee, Spike. *When the Levees Broke: A Requiem in Four Acts*. New York: 40 Acres and a Mule Filmworks, 2006. DVD.

Lixenberg, Dana. *The Last Days of Shishmaref*. Edam and Rotterdam, Netherlands: Paradox/Episode Publishing, 2008.

Lonetree, Amy. *Decolonizing Museums: Representing Native America in National and Tribal Museums*. Chapel Hill: University of North Carolina Press, 2012.

"Lora Ann Chaisson, United Houma Nation Tribal Member." YouTube video, 3:25. Posted August 26, 2010, by Bridge the Gulf Project. http://www.youtube.com/watch?v=FXWUhIle-L4.

Lord, Nancy. *Early Warming: Crisis and Response in the Climate-Changed North*. Berkeley, CA: Counterpoint, 2012.

Louisiana Coastal Wetlands Conservation and Restoration Task Force and the Wetlands Conservation and Restoration Authority. *Coast 2050: Toward a Sustainable Coastal Louisiana*. Baton Rouge: Louisiana Department of Natural Resources, 1998.

Lukacs, Martin. "New Brunswick Fracking Protests Are the Frontline of a Democratic Fight." *Guardian*, October 21, 2013

MacKenzie, Kent, writer and dir. *The Exiles*. 1961. Los Angeles, CA: Milestone Films, 2008. DVD.

Marino, Elizabeth. "The Long History of Environmental Migration: Assessing Vulnerability Construction and Obstacles to Successful Relocation in Shishmaref, Alaska." *Global Environmental Change* 22 (2012): 374–81.

Maristuen-Rodakowski, Julie. "The Turtle Mountain Reservation in North Dakota: Its History as Depicted in Louise Erdrich's *Love Medicine* and *The Beet Queen*." *American Indian Culture and Research Journal* 12 (1988): 33–48.

Martin, Michel. "Native American Group Hit Hard by Oil Spill." National Public Radio, June 3, 2010. http://www.npr.org/templates/story/story.php?storyId=127405886.

Martin, Robert J. "The Village of Kivalina Is Falling into the Sea: Should CERCLA Section 9626(b) Be Available to Move the Village from Harm's Way?" *Environmental and Earth Law Journal (EELJ)* 1.2 (2012): 1–32.

McClintock, Anne. "The Angel of Progress: Pitfalls of the Term 'Post-Colonialism.'" *Social Text* 31/32 (1992): 84–98.

McKay, James. "'That Awkwardness Is Important': An Interview with Diane Glancy." In *The Salt Companion to Diane Glancy*, edited by James McKay. London: Salt Publishing, 2010.

McMains, Frank. "The United Houma Nation, Staying Afloat." *Indian Country Today Media Network*, October 6, 2011. http://indiancountrytodaymedianetwork.com/2011/10/06/united-houma-nation-staying-afloat-57153.

Meyer, Melissa L. *The White Earth Tragedy: Ethnicity and Dispossession at a Minnesota Anishinaabe Reservation, 1889–1920.* Lincoln: University of Nebraska Press, 1994.

Mihesuah, Devon Abbott. *Indigenous American Women, Decolonization, Empowerment, Activism.* Lincoln: University of Nebraska Press, 2003.

Mooney, James. *Myths of the Cherokee.* Washington, D.C.: Smithsonian Institution, Bureau of American Ethnography, 1900.

Murphy, Patrick D. "Damning Damming Modernity: The Destructive Role of Megadams." *Tamkang Review* 42.1 (2011): 27–40.

NANA Regional Corporation, Inc. "Kivalina Village Profile." http://nana.com/files/pdf-bios/NANA-VillageProfile-Kivalina.pdf.

The National, CBC News. "Countdown to Friday: Explaining Idle No More." YouTube video, 18:14. Posted January 8, 2013, by *The National.* http://www.youtube.com/watch?v=sSdY_FVsGgo.

Navajo Nation. "Resolution of the Navajo Nation Council, Amending Title 1 of the NavajoNation Code to Recognize the Fundamental Laws of the Diné." http://www.navajocourts.org/resolutions.htm.

Niezen, Ronald. *Defending the Land: Sovereignty and Forest Life in James Bay Cree Society.* 2nd ed. Upper Saddle River, NJ: Pearson Education, Inc., 2009.

Noori, Margaret. "Beshaabiiag G'Gikenmaaigowag: Comets of Knowledge." In *Centering Anishinaabeg Studies: Understanding the World Through Stories,* edited by Jill Doerfler, Niigaanwewidam James Sinclair, and Heidi Kiiwetinepinesiik Stark, 35–60. East Lansing: Michigan State University Press, 2013.

Norgren, Jill. *The Cherokee Cases: The Confrontation of Law and Politics.* New York: McGraw Hill, Inc., 1996.

Ojibwe People's Dictionary, The. Created and updated by the Department of American Indian Studies and university libraries at the University of Minnesota. http://ojibwe.lib.umn.edu/.

Otis, D. S. *The Dawes Act and the Allotment of Indian Lands.* Norman: University of Oklahoma Press, 1973.

Owens, Louis. *I Hear the Train: Inventions, Reflections, Refractions.* Norman: University of Oklahoma Press, 2001.

———. *Mixedblood Messages: Literature, Film, Family, Place.* Norman: University of Oklahoma Press, 1998.

Perdue, Theda. *Cherokee Women: Gender and Culture Change, 1700–1835.* Lincoln: University of Nebraska Press, 1998.

———, and Michael D. Green. *The Cherokee Nation and the Trail of Tears.* New York: Viking Press, 2007.

————, and Michael D. Green, eds. *The Cherokee Removal: A Brief History with Documents*. Boston, MA: Bedford Books of St. Martin's Press, 1995.

Peterson, Nancy J. "History, Postmodernism, and Louise Erdrich's *Tracks*." *PMLA* 109 (1994): 982–94.

Picard, Andre. "James Bay II." *Amicus Journal* (Fall 1990): 10–16.

Powell, Dylan. "The 24 Hour Elsipogtog Raid Timeline." October 23, 2013. http://dylanxpowell.com/2013/10/23/the-24-hour-elsipogtog-raid-timeline/.

Press, Jordan, and Michael Woods. "Idle No More Movement 'Different' from Anything the Government Had Ever Seen Before, Documents Reveal." *Vancouver Sun*, April 10, 2013.

Prince, Hugh. *Wetlands of the American Midwest: A Historical Geography of Changing Attitudes*. Chicago, IL, and London: University of Chicago Press, 1997.

Pungowiyi, Caleb. "Native Observations of Change in the Marine Environment of the Bering Strait Region." *National Oceanic and Atmospheric Administration Arctic Theme Page*. http://www.arctic.noaa.gov/essay_pungowiyi.html.

Ramirez, Renya K. *Native Hubs: Culture, Community, and Belonging in Silicon Valley and Beyond*. Durham, NC: Duke University Press, 2007.

Ratner, Lizzy. "A Brief Story of Dispossession, American-Style—and What You Can Do About It." *Mondoweiss: The War of Ideas in the Middle East*, November 30, 2011. http://mondoweiss.net/2011/11/a-brief-story-of-dispossession-american-style-%E2%80%93-and-what-you-can-do-about-it.html.

Reed, Denise, and Lee Wilson. "Coast 2050: A New Approach to Restoration of Louisiana Coastal Wetlands." *Physical Geography* 25.1 (2004): 4–21.

Reed, T. V. "Toward an Environmental Justice Ecocriticism." In *The Environmental Justice Reader: Politics, Poetics, and Pedagogy*, edited by Joni Adamson, Mei Mei Evans, and Rachel Stein. Tucson: University of Arizona Press, 2002.

Regan, Sheila. "Idle No More Flash Roundy Fills Mall of America Rotunda." *Twin Cities Daily Planet*, December 29, 2012. http://www.tcdailyplanet.net/news/2012/12/30/idle-no-more-flash-roundy-mall-america.

Richardson, Boyce. *Strangers Devour the Land*. 1974. Reprint, White River Junction, VT: Chelsea Green Publishing Company, 1991.

Richland, Justin. *Arguing with Tradition: The Language of Law in Hopi Tribal Court*. Chicago, IL: University of Chicago Press, 2008.

Rifkin, Mark. "Representing the Cherokee Nation: Subaltern Studies and Native American Sovereignty." *boundary 2* 32.3 (2005): 47–80.

Roberts, J. Timmons, and Melissa M. Toffolon-Weiss. *Chronicles from the Environmental Justice Frontline*. Cambridge, MA: Cambridge University Press, 2001.

Robichaux, Brenda Dardar. Testimony. "House Committee on Natural Resources Oversight Hearing Gulf of Mexico: A Focus on Community Recovery and New Response Technology." April 18, 2011.

———. "We Like to Think Houma Women Are Very Strong." Ms. Foundation for Women Profile. In *The Women of Katrina: How Gender, Race, and Class Matter in an American Disaster*, edited by Emmanuel David and Elaine Enarson, 43–46. Nashville, TN: Vanderbilt University Press, 2012.

Rojas, Rick. "Idaho Tribe Files Suit to Halt Megaload Headed to Tar Sands." *Los Angeles Times*, August 9, 2013. http://articles.latimes.com/2013/aug/09/nation/la-na-nn-nez-perce-megaload-lawsuit-20130809.

———. "Judge Rules against 'Megaloads' of Tar Sands Equipment in Idaho." *Los Angeles Times*, September 13, 2013. http://www.latimes.com/nation/la-na-mega-load-20130914-story.html.

———. "Tribal Activists Block Shipment through Idaho Wilderness." *Los Angeles Times*, August 7, 2013. http://articles.latimes.com/2013/aug/07/nation/la-na-0808-tar-sands-20130808.

Rosenthal, Nicholas G. *Reimagining Indian Country: Native American Migration and Identity in Twentieth-Century Los Angeles*. Chapel Hill: University of North Carolina Press, 2012.

Ross, Loretta J. "A Feminist Perspective on Katrina." In *The Women of Katrina: How Gender, Race, and Class Matter in an American Disaster*, edited by Emmanuel David and Elaine Enarson, 15–24. Nashville, TN: Vanderbilt University Press, 2012.

Rozelle, Page. "The Teller and the Tale: History and the Oral Tradition in Elizabeth Cook-Lynn's *Aurelia: A Crow Creek Trilogy*." *American Indian Quarterly* 25.2 (2001): 203–15.

Rozema, Vicki, ed. *Voices from the Trail of Tears*. Winston-Salem, NC: John F. Blair, Publisher, 2003.

Ruppel, Kristin T. *Unearthing Indian Land: Living with the Legacies of Allotment*. Tucson: University of Arizona Press, 2008.

Rushton, Steve. "Steve Rushton Interviews Sylvia McAdam." Radio interview, 23:17. January 28, 2013. *Occupy Radio LDN*. http://www.mixcloud.com/markweaver5015/idle-no-more-steve-rushton-interviews-sylvia-mcadam.

Sam-Cromarty, Margaret. "Family Closeness: Will James Bay Be Only a Memory for My Grandchildren?" In *Defending Mother Earth: Native American Perspectives on Environmental Justice*, edited by Jace Weaver. Maryknoll, NY: Orbis Books, 1996.

Schlichting, Rebekka. "Native Americans, Supporters Put on Flash Mob Demonstration in South Park for Idle No More." *Lawrence Journal-World*,

January 12, 2013. http://www2.ljworld.com/news/2013/jan/12/hundreds-native-americans-flash-mob-south-park-idl/.

Seager, Joni. "Noticing Gender (or Not) in Disasters." In *The Women of Katrina: How Gender, Race, and Class Matter in an American Disaster*, edited by Emmanuel David and Elaine Enarson, 7–9. (Nashville, TN: Vanderbilt University, 2012).

Sevareid, Eric. *Canoeing with the Cree*. 1930. Reprint, New York: Borealis Books, 2005.

Shanley, Kathryn W. "Thoughts on Indian Feminism." In *A Gathering of Spirit: A Collection by North American Indian Women*, edited by Beth Brant, 213–16. Ithaca, NY: Firebrand Books, 1984.

Shearer, Christine. *Kivalina: A Climate Change Story*. Chicago, IL: Haymarket Books, 2011.

Siegel, Robert, and Melissa Block. "Profile: Remembering the Navajo Long Walk." *All Things Considered*. National Public Radio, June 14, 2005.

Silko, Leslie Marmon. "Here's an Odd Artifact for the Fairy-Tale Shelf." Review of *The Beet Queen* by Louise Erdrich. *Impact/Albuquerque Journal*, October 8, 1986.

———. *Yellow Woman and a Beauty of the Spirit*. New York: Simon & Schuster, 1996.

Smith, Andrea. *Conquest: Sexual Violence and American Indian Genocide*. Cambridge, MA: South End Press, 2005.

Solomon, Gina M., and Sarah Janssen. "Health Effects of the Gulf Oil Spill." *The Journal of the American Medical Association* 304.10 (2010): 1118–19.

Stacks, Geoffrey. "A Defiant Cartography: Linda Hogan's *Solar Storms*." *Mosaic* 43.1 (2010): 161–77.

Tapahonso, Luci. "In 1864." In *Sáanii Dahataał: The Women Are Singing*. Tucson: University of Arizona Press, 1993.

Tarter, Jim. "'Dreams of Earth': Place, Multiethnicity, and Environmental Justice in Linda Hogan's *Solar Storms*." In *Reading Under the Sign of Nature: New Essays in Ecocriticism*, edited by John Tallmadge and Henry Harrington, 128–47. Salt Lake City: University of Utah Press, 2000.

Teuton, Christopher B. *Deep Waters: The Textual Continuum in American Indian Literature*. Lincoln: University of Nebraska Press, 2010.

Tidwell, Mike. *Bayou Farewell: The Rich Life and Tragic Death of Louisiana's Cajun Coast*. New York: Vintage Books, 2004.

Tohe, Laura. "There Is No Word for Feminism in My Language." *Wicazo Sa Review* 15.2 (2000): 103–10.

Tsosie, Rebecca. "Indigenous People and Environmental Justice: The Impact of Climate Change." *University of Colorado Law Review* 78 (2007): 1625.

Twilley, Robert. "Interview with Robert Twilley." *WaterMarks: Louisiana Coastal Wetlands Planning, Protection and Restoration News*, February 22, 2003.

"Unheard Voices from the Gulf Coast: United Houma Nation." YouTube video, 3:23. Posted June 25, 2010, by greenforall. http://www.youtube.com/watch?v=of3qEhDbi1Y.

United Houma Nation. http://www.unitedhoumanation.org.

"United Houma Nation Youth Media Lab." YouTube video, 2:15. Posted August 13, 2010, by Bridge the Gulf Project. http://www.youtube.com/watch?v=wYT6-Bftmig.

United States Environmental Protection Agency. "Alaska Impacts and Adaptation." http://www.epa.gov/climatechange/impacts-adaptation/alaska.html#ImpactsAlaska.

Van Gelder, Sarah. "Speaking with the Founders of Idle No More." *Huffington Post Canada*, February 21, 2013. http://www.huffingtonpost.ca/sarah-van-gelder/idle-no-more-founders_b_2708644.html.

———. "Why Canada's Indigenous Uprising Is About All of Us." *Yes! Magazine*, February 7, 2013. http://www.yesmagazine.org/issues/how-cooperatives-are-driving-the-new-economy/why-canada2019s-indigenous-uprising-is-about-all-of-us.

Van Heerden, Ivor, and Mike Bryan. *The Storm: What Went Wrong and Why During Hurricane Katrina—The Inside Story from One Louisiana Scientist.* New York: Viking Press, 2006.

Van Meter McCoy, Sondra, and Jan Hults. *1001 Kansas Place Names.* Lawrence: University of Kansas Press, 1989.

Vizenor, Gerald. "Minnesota Chippewa: Woodland Treaties to Tribal Bingo." *American Indian Quarterly* 13.2 (1989): 30–57.

Waldram, James B. *As Long as the Rivers Run: Hydroelectric Development and Native Communities in Western Canada.* Winnipeg: University of Manitoba Press, 1988.

Warhus, Mark. *Another America: Native American Maps and the History of Our Land.* New York: St. Martin's Press, 1997.

Warrior, Robert Allen. *The People and the Word: Reading Native Nonfiction.* Minneapolis: University of Minnesota Press, 2005.

———. *Tribal Secrets: Recovering American Indian Intellectual Traditions.* Minneapolis: University of Minnesota Press, 1995.

Washburn, Wilcomb E. *The Assault on Indian Tribalism: The General Allotment Law (Dawes Act) of 1887.* Philadelphia, PA: J. B. Lippincott Company, 1975.

Washington, Mary Helen. "Disturbing the Peace: What Happens to American Studies If You Put African American Studies at the Center?: Presidential

Address to the American Studies Association, October 29, 1997." *American Quarterly* 50.1 (Mar. 1998): 1–23.

Weaver, Jace. *Defending Mother Earth: Native American Perspectives on Environmental Justice*. Maryknoll, NY: Orbis Books, 1996.

———. *Notes from a Miner's Canary: Essays on the State of Native America*. Albuquerque: University of New Mexico Press, 2010.

———. *Other Words: American Indian Literature, Law, and Culture*. Norman: University of Oklahoma Press, 2001.

———. "Splitting the Earth: First Utterances and Pluralist Separatism." In *American Indian Literary Nationalism*, edited by Jace Weaver, Craig Womack, and Robert Warrior, 1–89. Albuquerque: University of New Mexico Press, 2005.

———. *That the People Might Live: Native American Literatures and Native American Communities*. New York: Oxford University Press, 1997.

Weibel-Orlando, Joan. *Indian Country, L.A.: Maintaining Ethnic Community in Complex Society*. Urbana: University of Illinois Press, 1991.

Weil, Richard H. "Destroying a Homeland: White Earth, Minnesota." *American Indian Culture and Research Journal* 13.2 (1989): 69–95.

Wells, Ken. "Collapsing Marsh Dwarfs BP Blowout as Ecological Disaster." *Bloomberg News*, August 17, 2010. http://www.bloomberg.com/news/2010-08-18/collapsing-louisiana-marsh-dwarfs-bp-oil-blowout-as-environmental-disaster.html.

Wexler, Laura. *Tender Violence: Domestic Visions in the Age of U.S. Imperialism*. Chapel Hill: University of North Carolina Press, 2000.

Willmott, Kevin, dir. *The Only Good Indian*. Written by Tom Carmody. Lawrence, KS: TLC Films, 2009.

Womack, Craig S. *Red on Red: Native American Literary Separatism*. Minneapolis: University of Minnesota Press, 1999.

Worster, Donald. *Rivers of Empire: Water, Aridity, and the Growth of the American West*. New York: Oxford University Press, 1992.

Young, Phyllis. "Beyond the Water Line." In *Defending Mother Earth: Native American Perspectives on Environmental Justice*, edited by Jace Weaver, 85–98. Maryknoll, NY: Orbis Books, 1996.

Youngbear-Tibbetts, Holly. "Without Due Process: The Alienation of Individual Trust Allotments of the White Earth Anishinaabeg." *American Indian Culture and Research Journal* 15.2 (1991): 93–138.

Zarembo, Alan. "An Alaskan Island Finds Itself Losing Ground." *Los Angeles Times*, November 25, 2007. http://articles.latimes.com/2007/nov/25/science/sci-kivalina25.

INDEX

Page numbers in italic text indicate illustrations.